A Brief History of
ST. PAUL'S SCHOOL
1856–1996

A Brief History of
ST. PAUL'S SCHOOL
1856–1996

AUGUST HECKSCHER

Introduction by Charles Scribner III

CONCORD, NEW HAMPSHIRE

Cataloging-in-Publication Data is on file with the Library of Congress.

EDITOR: Alan Neidlinger Hall
BOOK AND COVER DESIGN: Jenny Jensen Greenleaf
FRONT COVER PHOTO: Dan Habib
MAP ILLUSTRATIONS: Richard Brooke Roberts '70

All photographs herein come from the archives of St. Paul's School, with the following exceptions: pages 12 and 43 courtesy New Hampshire Historical Society;
page 20 (top) from Bliss Perry, *Richard Henry Dana, 1851–1931*, and (bottom)
from Mark A. de Wolfe Howe, *John Jay Chapman and His Letters;* pages 24 and
53 courtesy Trinity College Library; pages 26 and 72 courtesy Mrs. Emily M.
Beck; page 31 from James Knox, *Henry Augustus Coit;* pages 46 and 61 from
John Davies, *The Legend of Hobie Baker;* page 59 courtesy Mrs. Richard Eaton;
pages 76 and 90 courtesy Roger W. Drury; pages 87 and 133 Toni Frissell; page
153 Tom Jones Photo; page 154 courtesy R. L. Dothard Associates; pages 161,
169, 171, 174, 175, 179, 180, 190, 192 Bradford Herzog; page 163, Alan N.
Hall; page 185, George Grove; page 189 (top) Deborah de Peyster, (bottom)
courtesy Marcia Matthews.

Printed in the United States of America on acid-free paper.

Contents

Introduction

by Charles Scribner III

As I was reading this new, updated edition of August Heckscher's history of St. Paul's—some fifteen years after the publication of the original edition—I recalled one of my favorite Latin mottos: *Non novum sed nove*—not something new, but something seen in a new way. As a tyro editor at Scribners in the late 1970s I had the privilege of working with August Heckscher on his now-classic volume *St. Paul's: The Life of a New England School*, which we published in time for the School's 125th Anniversary. Several decades earlier my grandfather had published Arthur Stanwood Pier's history of our alma mater in 1934, the year my father entered as a second former. I suppose that explains why we were given the honor of producing the new history. In any event, my father had asked me to oversee its publication, and I proceeded, I now confess, more out of duty than anticipation or excitement. I was soon to discover—upon receiving the manuscript—how wrong I had been in my initial response.

August Heckscher was, to be sure, the perfect author for this book. A most distinguished alumnus, he had served as student editor of the *Horae Scholasticae* as a prelude to becoming, years later, chief editorial writer of *The New York Herald Tribune* and the director of the Twentieth Century Fund. His public career included service as cultural advisor in the

Kennedy administration and parks commissioner and chief of cultural affairs for New York City under Mayor John Lindsay, another distinguished alumnus of SPS. Among his earlier books were *The Public Happiness,* an examination of the American political condition, and studies on urban themes including *Alive in the City, Open Spaces,* and *When La Guardia Was Mayor.*

Heckscher served as a SPS Trustee for twenty-six years, and I well remembered from my student days his visit to the school as a Conroy Fellow in 1967. He represented the aesthetic conscience of the Board during that period of architectural expansion under Matthew Warren. (One faculty wit, I recall, coined the epigram "Augie Heckscher, give us Architecture!") So he was ideally matched with his subject and would bring to it both insight and eloquence. Still, I feared, his commission had been to write an authorized, official institutional history and his book would inevitably be constrained by the limits of the genre. (In my view, institutional history was to history what military music was to music.) I was totally unprepared for the result.

"Every school is a commonwealth in miniature," wrote a St. Paul's student over a century ago. In chronicling the life of our miniature commonwealth in Millville from its pre-Civil War founding to the present day, Heckscher wove a narrative as engaging as a work of fiction, his characters as colorful and memorable as those of a novel. He produced a vivid and resonant work of literature, a non-fiction counterpart, as it were, to Louis Auchincloss' *The Rector of Justin.* His intimate account of life in this unique community broadened into a fresh view of American social and cultural history. But then, St. Paul's was ever a beacon that shines far beyond its local domain. Among the many tributes for this book—and there were many indeed—the one I still cherish above all is a letter I received from the former rector Matthew Warren, then already a decade into his retirement:

My dear Charlie:

You are a generous and thoughtful friend to send me your advanced copy of August Heckscher's superb book. He and you extend greater Powers to this elderly, arthritic gent—but I love it all—than he deserves. The years at SPS were fascinating, deeply involving both my wife and me but ever so rewarding. Now this beautiful book graces our declining years and, coming from you, it adds warmth and personal affection which I reciprocate eagerly and quickly. Bless you and all your works...

Becky joins in affectionate gratitude for the book. We sat down at once and began reading it aloud. Reading to each other began on our wedding trip and has stayed with us, thank God, ever since.

Our love to you and your family—

Gratefully,
Matt M. Warren

No best seller has meant more to me than this book, for it engendered a magnificent offspring, Heckscher's peerless biography of Woodrow Wilson, published a decade later. It was his book on St. Paul's that alone inspired that new commission. What new subject for a book by this gifted author could adequately embrace those interwoven SPS themes of educational reform, idealism, religious conviction, vision, and, yes, raw politics and human conflict? As an unrepentant Princetonian, I could think of only one: Woodrow Wilson. This "brief" assignment was to span a full ten years of research and writing. Halfway through it, my father sent me a note: "I don't know which is less likely: that the author will live to finish it or that I will live to read it." (Happily, he was wrong on both counts.) It was worth the wait, for its publication coincided—almost providentially—with President Bush's recapitulation of the Wilsonian "New World Order." The critical praise was resounding. Heckscher set a new standard for presidential biography, one that is consistent with his approach to St. Paul's. My favorite letter—and a most revealing one—was received from a former U. S. President, who turned out to be a more ardent Wilsonian than I had ever dreamed:

Dear Mr. Scribner,

As one who has read most of the biographies of Woodrow Wilson, I would rate August Heckscher's at the top of the list. He is obviously an admirer of Wilson, but lets the reader see his faults as well as his virtues. My impression after reading the book from cover to cover was that Wilson was a great leader who won great victories and suffered great defeats. But the key word is great—Wilson was a great President, and the Heckscher biography does justice to his greatness by letting us see the whole man. In fact, an appropriate subtitle for the book might be "The Real Wilson."

Sincerely,
Richard Nixon

The same, I submit, might be said of Heckscher's new, concise history of St. Paul's—"The Real St. Paul's." By highlighting the past challenges, achievements, dreams and struggles, bringing our story right up to the present day, he casts new and much needed light on our current goals, controversies, debates, accomplishments, and hopes. *Nihil sub sole novum!*
The energy that fuels the life of St. Paul's is nothing less than a powerful fusion of community and curriculum, and the impact it makes on a student's memory and future cannot be overestimated. No day passes without some incident, some impression, some insight from those four years spent in Millville bubbling up into consciousness. My own memories of St. Paul's are more vivid than anything that came before or after in my education.
I know I must share with countless alumni those memories that are the stuff of low comedy, though often containing a

salutary lesson, such as the time I plugged my Bunsen burner hose into a water faucet in Mr. Gillespie's chemistry class. I turned it on and a jet of liquid shot up and hit the ceiling. Liquid gas! I panicked, shut it off, blew out my match. We had just narrowly escaped being blown up, yet Mr. Gillespie seemed remarkably calm and bemused. "Eh, Scribner," he asked, "did you have any trouble lighting it?" Moral: don't panic, and don't leap to conclusions—a lesson as applicable to the humanities as to science.

On a more contemplative plane, I recall a religion class in which we were reading and doing an exegesis of St. Mark's Gospel in the original koine Greek (one of the spiritual rewards of struggling through years of ancient Greek at St. Paul's). Our teacher, David Barry, was illustrating a great subtlety in the Greek text describing baptism, something that English was not quite supple enough to duplicate. We have an active and a passive voice, that is all: you hit me; I am hit. But the Greeks had a third, a "middle" voice, for their verbs, something that may convey a passive experience in which the subject initiates the act and receives the effect of it.

The King James Bible says that the people of Judea and Jerusalem "were all baptized" by John in the river Jordan. But it was not simply a passive act. They had taken the initiative and "went out to him" to subject themselves to John in this act of repentance. So St. Mark cast the verb in the middle voice, between and combining active and passive. With a flash of insight Mr. Barry suggested that we might translate ἐβαπτίζοντο "got themselves baptized"—they got themselves baptized by John in the river Jordan. A bit colloquial, "got" or "get" is a blunt Old Norse word that sounded somewhat crude, but it worked. It precisely conveyed the nuance of the Greek middle voice and St. Mark's intention in describing the significance of the event.

I suppose that the reason this episode in translating a single word looms so large in my memory is that, in a very simple way, it encapsulates the St. Paul's experience. I no longer remember my Greek vocabulary, and I certainly cannot conjugate the middle voice, but that grammatical Greek subtlety captures the essence of our learning experience at St. Paul's. It was both active and passive, as we got ourselves educated (middle voice). Above all, it was—and is—collaborative and communal. It transcended the grid of the daily schedule, as curricular and extracurricular blended together; and it has extended well beyond the boundaries both of four academic calendars and of that idyllic campus, as indeed the school motto says it should: *Ea discamus in terris quorum scientia perseveret in coelis*. "Let us learn those things on earth the knowledge of which may continue in heaven."

Some years ago, I wrote a letter to one of my favorite authors, Graham Greene. I had first been exposed to Greene's religious mysteries as a third former watching an SPS production of his haunting play *The Potting Shed*. It is about a young man, the son of a famous atheist, who has hanged himself and is resurrected by the desperate prayer of his uncle, a priest who barters his most precious possession, his faith in God, for the boy's life. A fellow Catholic, I later felt a special debt to Greene's work and asked him to write a book about his personal theology and views on the Church. He politely but pointedly declined, saying that he did not want to write anything on Catholicism and the Church in an essay. "I would rather that people dug out my ideas from my fiction," he explained to me. That struck a chord, for it was precisely what we were trained and encouraged to do at St. Paul's: to dig out ideas from our books, from our teachers, from each other.

I should like to conclude these introductory reflections with a morsel of fiction, a little story or parable that my father told me when I was a student at SPS and that he himself had been told some thirty years earlier by Dr. Drury in Chapel. (Dr. Drury's son Roger, who was a classmate of August Heckscher's and fellow editor of the *Horae Scholasticae*, recently confirmed the source, saying that it was the one sermon he best remembers being given at St. Paul's by his father.)

Once upon a time a young prince was making a journey alone on horseback to another kingdom. He had come a long way and he had a long way to go. One night as he was crossing a stream he heard a commanding voice call to him out of the darkness: "Stop and fill up your saddle bags with the sand of this stream." The young prince reined in his horse for an instant and deliberated. He was awed by the voice and he wanted to obey, but he was also impatient to ride on. So all he did was to reach down and snatch up a handful of sand from the bottom of the stream, put it in his pocket and gallop off on his way.

The next morning he remembered the stream and the voice and the sand. Out of curiosity he reached into his pocket and lo and behold it was filled with diamonds. And so, as the story goes, the young prince was both glad and sorry. He was glad that he had stopped and taken some sand and he was sorry that he had been impatient and not taken more.

It is the common experience—and joy—of both teachers and students alike at St. Paul's to discover, sometimes years later, that what first appeared as sand sparkles as diamonds.

Acknowledgements

First, thanks to the Trustees. When the original edition of *St. Paul's: The Life of a New England School* (published in 1980 by Charles Scribner's Sons) began to run low, they asked me to bring the book up to date in preparation for a reprinting. I was reluctant to add chapters to a work that, for better or worse, stood as a whole, and countered with the suggestion that I abridge the earlier version and add an account of the most recent years. In this they acquiesced. The present volume is the result.

In earlier chapters I have often plagiarized myself, yet with sufficient reconsideration, I hope, to set the whole tale in the perspective of this century's closing years. I have omitted citation of sources as well as a bibliography. These are readily available in the earlier volume. In the later chapters sources are self-evident or consist largely of confidential interviews.

Trustees Edmund P. Pillsbury first worked with me in determining the scope and nature of the book, and Charles Scribner III has been generous not only in contributing the Introduction but in reading the manuscript with care and advising on matters of design and production. Walker Lewis, President of the Board, has been unfailing in his support throughout.

Among others to whom I owe much are: Dr. J. C. Douglas Marshall, head of the St. Paul's classics department and authority on the school's history; Alan N. Hall, master wordsmith, my editor, efficient beyond thanks in helping me through the last stages of the work; Richard Cowan, vice rector, enthusiastic pro moter of the project; and Rosemarie Cassels-Brown and Robert Rettew, former and present chief librarians of Ohrstrom Library. Without the generous help of José Ordoñez, finding the photographs would have been much more difficult. Jenny Greenleaf's handsome design of the book speaks for itself.

Many at the school, students and faculty, who have allowed me to interview them must forgive a silent and inclusive acknowledgment.

Two rectors unknown to St. Paul's when my earlier history was completed have been most helpful. Charles H. Clark looked back with me, unhurriedly and reflectively, over his tenure. David V. Hicks, amid many burdens and distractions, answered all my questions candidly and made crucial documents available. During two week-long visits he extended to me every resource of the school— and more than that, every mark of hospitality and kindness.

AUGUST HECKSCHER
High Loft, Maine
July 1995

PART ONE

1

The Beginning

1856

St. Paul's School, in Concord, New Hampshire, is today a place of more than 2,000 acres; an aggregation of some hundred structures containing a population, all told, of approximately 1,000 people. It is a community inextricably linked with the contemporary world and with the surrounding countryside; yet it stands somewhat apart, not quite of its own time in its conscious search for excellence, its adherence to long-ingrained ideals of learning and work, and its hope (like most hopes not always fulfilled!) of achieving a perfected communal existence. How St. Paul's came into being, the vicissitudes of its growth and development up to this point, is the subject of this brief history.

The beginning has the quality of myth, though the myth is well substantiated. On April 3, 1856—five years before the American Civil War—a carriage whose passengers consisted of a twenty-four-year-old schoolmaster, his bride of seven days, two boys, and a dog drove down into the gentle valley where the hamlet of Millville lay between ponds and the meandering Turkey River. A third boy awaited them at the large house which had been the country seat of George Cheyne Shattuck, a well-known Boston physician. Chores were immediately assigned to the three boys.[1] The day ended with the Rector reading a story

---

1. The three boys, two of whom were sons of Dr. Shattuck, were immediately given tasks which in an amusingly symbolic way reflect characteristic aspects of the school, enduring throughout its history. The first was assigned a composition on "Strength of Purpose"—the moral quality; the second, a composition on "Adventures of a Lion"—the quality of action; the third was allowed to go fishing—the quality of humane leisure and relatedness to nature.

and evening prayers. "It was a small beginning...but all things, large or small, must have a beginning." So wrote the schoolmaster, the first rector, Henry Augustus Coit, when the school had reached its first quarter century.

St. Paul's originated in Dr. Shattuck's desire to educate his sons in a place where natural beauty—"green fields and trees (as he wrote), streams and ponds...flowers and minerals"—could play a vital part in a boy's education; and where an affectionate family atmosphere would prevail. His own schooling had been at Round Hill in Northampton, Massachusetts, where these conditions had been cultivated. Established in 1823 by the future historian George Bancroft, Round Hill had been much influenced by Swiss and German experiments in progressive education. It came to an end after a brief existence, but Dr. Shattuck retained memories of its humane and liberal regimen.

Having organized a board of trustees, Shattuck turned over to them his country home and its adjacent farm. The Board ap-

The Founder, Dr. George Cheyne Shattuck, Jr.

Henry Augustus Coit, the first Rector.

pointed as rector a clergyman of twenty-four years who had been a student in a school similar to Round Hill in its idealistic and experimental nature, but one striking an additional note: that of an intense religious life, with an emphasis on ceremony and ritual, symbolism and tradition. This was the Flushing Institute, of Flushing, Long Island, New York. Its founder and commanding genius was the German-born William Augustus Muhlenberg.

Thus present at the founding of St. Paul's were two potent influences— belief in the beneficence of nature imparted by Round Hill, and a kind of unworldliness and a religious faith imparted by the Flushing Institute. St. Paul's has been at its best when these two influences—that of nature and that of faith—have both been at work; when the memory of its founder, George Shattuck, and of its first rector, Henry Coit, have together shaped its course.

It will be a surprise to many, and perhaps a disappointment to some, to learn that St. Paul's was not established on English models. Later the school would adopt many English customs, but the English public schools of the early nineteenth century were in a deplorable condition, scholastically lax, with student bodies prone to licentiousness and rebellion. Far from wanting to create in the United States a new Rugby or a new Eton, the founders of St. Paul's were bent on creating an institution at once more genial than they, and more austere.

The founding of St. Paul's did not run altogether smoothly. Before turning to the young Coit—not with entire enthusiasm (they worried about his immaturity and his lack of experience)— the Trustees in their search for a rector made several false steps. Indeed they almost despaired of finding a suitable man. They first chose as rector a clergyman of Bangor, Maine, who turned out to be pathologically insecure and subject to fits of despondency. He declined, after much hesitation, the post to which he had already been elected. "Well—it is as it is," wrote a member of the Board to Dr. Shattuck. "It may all be for the best."

So indeed it was; for in finally settling on Henry Coit the Trustees chose a man cut out to be a great schoolmaster, one of those characters rare in any generation who find themselves perfectly suited to fulfill a great work begun in their youth. For almost thirty-nine years Coit ruled over St. Paul's, authoritative, pious, a figure inspiring awe and leaving with those who came under his rule vivid memories and affections. He could, for all his severity, be touchingly modest and surprisingly compassionate, and somehow he encouraged his young charges to dream dreams and to follow their own lights.

2

The School Grows

1856–1865

❧

Through most of its history, St. Paul's has seemed physically remote, situated in a mountainous realm of its own. The town of Concord was, it is true, only 65 miles north of Boston, but they were miles that set it well apart, not only from Boston but even from such manufacturing centers as Manchester and Nashua to the south. Capital of a state that sent good, solid Franklin Pierce to the White House, Concord prided itself on its skilled labor, its spirit of enterprise, and its capacity to strike a good deal—whether in the shops along Main Street or at the State House and in the smoky rooms of the Eagle Hotel.

Around Concord the land was rich in natural features. Quarries, abandoned shortly before St. Paul's was founded, provided natural swimming places. With its views of New Hampshire's Franconia Mountains to the north and of Monadnock to the southwest, Jerry Hill, not far from the school, provided a tempting climb for man or boy. Long Pond, a crystal sheet of water fed by pure springs from the surrounding hills, abounded in perch and pickerel. Big Turkey Pond (today the school's rowing site) fed the ponds at the heart of Millville and wandered off into the Turkey River, once the source of power for numerous small mills. This varied countryside, with its woods and farms, provided an unfailing attraction to students of St. Paul's and fortified its sense of being in a world of its own.

Over this domain played a climate of unusual severity and changefulness. It was a climate, asserted the local historian, "fa-

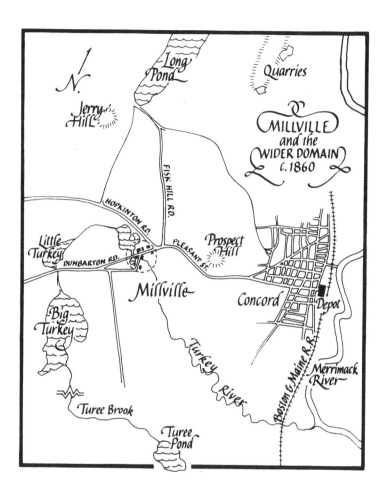

vorable to health and longevity." Winter set in early, with ponds frozen solid by Thanksgiving and deep snows lasting well into March. Temperatures regularly sank to twenty-five degrees below zero and on two occasions reached records of thirty-seven below. At the school during its first fifty years ther-mometer readings taken at three different times of the day were painstakingly recorded for posterity. In addition, storms broke with particular force, and floods and droughts were common. Celestial displays unusual in their brilliance occurred, and earthquakes ranging from mild to moderate.

The little band of settlers in Millville experienced a first winter harsh even by Concord's standards. They slid, slipped, and fell along the icy road on their way to church, and water froze in the rooms where they slept. Yet the school took shape and a lively scholastic life was established. It was essentially an expanded family, a clergyman and his wife living with a few boys in a large country house. From the beginning, however, it was more than that. A vision of the future school animated Dr. Coit, as he established the forms and traditions of a true community.

The daily routine was rigorous. A bell woke the boys at five; breakfast, followed by prayers, was at six. Classes ran from seven to one-thirty, after which a dinner (one hopes it was a hearty dinner) followed at one-thirty. The students were then free until tea at six-thirty. Study, stories and parlor games, finally evening prayers, brought them to the bedtime hour of nine.

In that first year (1856-1857) the Rector accompanied the boys on expeditions by coach—the passengers warmed by furs, shawls, and buffalo robes—to such nearby villages as Hopkinton or Dunbarton; or out to Canterbury, where a still-populous and vital colony of Shakers entertained the visitors with the kind of good food that compensated for their otherwise severe habits. Again, the boys were taken to the factory where the famous Concord coaches, destined to travel the world over, were being manufactured. On July 23—for the scholastic year was long in the early years, and vacations short—Dr. Coit decreed a holiday to mark Dr. Shattuck's birthday. "Long may the day be celebrated in his honor," exclaimed the Rector. And thus it was indeed to be, for placed in June, and under the name of "Anniversary," it became a principal event in the school year, even when later generations forgot altogether what it was they were celebrating.

At the end of that first year scholastic honors were awarded and a scene from *The Merchant of Venice* was staged. After the quiet festivities the Rector sat alone, in a reflective mood. By the next day, he wrote in his diary, all would be gone, and old walls would echo with faint footsteps. "We hope that no boy goes away from here unimproved," he added—words that to this day are repeated in the school's last-night prayer.

During the next few years the fledgling school began to take the form of an ongoing institution. The Civil War was a watershed even for Millville, with St. Paul's still a family at its close, as in a sense it would remain, but with a growing list of students, with well-established customs, and with masters coming to share the Rector's burdens.

Important in making plain that St. Paul's was intended to endure was the construction of the first new building. This was a chapel (now known as the "Old Chapel") donated by Dr. Shattuck and designed by the Boston architect George Snell. It stood just east of the School House and during its first years was a simple rectangle in form. With appropriate ceremonies the cornerstone was laid on St. Peter's Day, June 29, 1858. Nineteen months later, on St. Paul's Day, the work was completed. Dr. Shattuck and a considerable group of friends came up from Boston. After the consecration service and a "light collation" all repaired to the nearby pond, including bishops and clergy, whom the boys pushed at high speed over the ice on sleds.

In 1864 the opening of the school was briefly delayed while major additions and rearrangements in the School House were being completed. By this time some of the students and faculty had their rooms in buildings of the original farm (the Shute Cottage, the Miller's Cottage), and the place was beginning to attain the scattered, village-like atmosphere of later years.

Among the first masters to arrive were John T. Wheeler, who at Christmas, 1861, composed the quaint Latin verses of Salve Mater, since sung by St. Paul's alumni at their gatherings. Thomas C. Valpey, a dull pedant in his time, has left his name on

*The Rector's wife,
Mary B. Coit.*

a school prize; and John Hargate, no intellectual light but a loyal aide to the Rector, has left his on one of the school's major buildings. Two men of a different caliber next arrived. These were Hall Harrison, and Dr. Coit's brother, Joseph Howland Coit. Both had been teaching at St. James College in Hagerstown, Maryland, which was in its way, like St. Paul's, an offspring of Muhlenberg's Flushing Institute. St. James was devastated by the Civil War and closed its doors, but its influence lived in the two men who now were to play so large a part at Millville.

Harrison had his eccentricities; he remained loyal to the Confederate cause and banned *Uncle Tom's Cabin* from the school library. But as a teacher he had temperament and style. He was a graceful writer and conversationalist and imparted to

The Merrimack River, looking north to Concord and the New Hampshire hills. A painting by Josiah Wolcott, 1847.

students a genuine love of literature. Joseph Coit, too, was a civilizing, stimulating presence. After graduation from St. James he had studied for two years at the Sorbonne in Paris. He brought to the school a sense of the larger world and a genial educational philosophy. Supplementing the Rector's gifts, he would in due course succeed him.

Two other masters, inseparable friends, deserve to be remembered among the St. Paul's "greats." James Carter Knox, a student in the 1860s, returned to the school as a handsome figure, pale and with long mustaches, always impeccably dressed. In these early days a sovereign teacher and a charmed musician, he trained an expert choir. But more than that, he led the boys in familiar songs and joined them in their sports. The school anthem, O Pray for the Peace of Jerusalem, was—along with the music for several other favorite hymns—composed by him.

Augustus M. Swift, also a student from the sixties, had spent a year in England at Dr. Coit's suggestion in the household of the Reverend Derwent Coleridge, son of the poet. There he studied the classics and perfected his musical and artistic gifts. When he returned to the school in 1872, he came like a fresh breeze—like "an April shower," as one of his con-

"They brought a fresh air to the school..."

Augustus M. Swift   *James C. Knox*

temporaries put it, falling upon Millville's Puritanical soil. He became as a son to the Rector; he was for many of the students almost an idol, as he coasted and skated with them—always debonair and cheerful—or sang at their gatherings in his fine baritone voice. By his gifts and by his example he brought an appreciation of the arts to St. Paul's.[1]

The outbreak of war had found the community in a patriotic fervor. Students raised flags and fired at least one small cannon. They built a fort in the woods, divided themselves into opposing forces, and fought with green apples for ammunition. A drillmaster came regularly to the school, and under his tutelage the boys attained what was described as "tolerable discipline" in the basic military arts. He soon enlisted, becoming one of Concord's first casualties when he fell from a railway car as it passed through New Jersey. In his honor, the school flag was lowered to half mast. The first St. Paul's boy to volunteer was Francis Lewis Abbot (SPS 1862), son of Concord's eminent coachmaker; and one St. Paul's student, William Hall Turner (SPS 1861), was killed fighting for the Confederacy.

For a while it appeared that the Rector would be drafted. "All things considered," as he liked to say, it was fortunate for the school that he was not. His genius was essential to its growth. At the war's end he was still in command, and St. Paul's advanced through the following decade to a unique place among American educational institutions.

---

1. In 1884 Swift died tragically of a sudden illness in Rome where, on leave from the school, he had gone on his honeymoon. Word of his passing devastated Millville. He is buried in the Protestant Cemetery in Rome.

3

Arcadian Times

1865–1875

The session of 1871–1872 saw the arrival of sixty new boys, the largest number up to that time. The school's facilities were crowded; the pond was overflowing after years of drought; the mill once more pursued its busy round. The Rector and the Trustees could well feel satisfaction with their work. Admission to St. Paul's was now becoming an enviable accomplishment, and letters of the period show every wile on the part of parents and sponsors of would-be entrants.

"You will find him a pleasant and docile pupil," wrote one of these; "He has no vices but needs only mental culture," wrote another. "I had hoped better things of him," adds a father of his son who was looking toward Harvard: "Perhaps after a year with you he may be willing to go to Trinity." Among those making such appeals were Samuel Seabury, a descendant of the first Episcopal bishop in America; Edward L. Godkin, editor of *The Nation*; and George William Curtis, editor of *Harper's*.

St. Paul's offered a smooth pathway into college; yet such was by no means its chief aim. Indeed at its start the school was much more concerned with preparing young men for life than for the colleges of that day. Then courses of study were hardly more advanced than those offered at Millville, and their student bodies were young and immature.

Of the first seventy students graduated from St. Paul's only five went to college. Unlike the academies such as Andover, Deerfield, and Exeter, or the later "feeder schools" like

15

The dam at Millville and the Miller's Cottage, the latter in its altered form.

Lawrenceville and Hotchkiss, St. Paul's did not care to adjust itself to the entrance requirements of other institutions. Its ideal of a liberal and humane curriculum, combined with religious training, active sports, and a richly developed community life, led the school along a path of its own. Besides, Dr. Coit did not approve of the Unitarian heresies at Harvard, the preferred choice for many of his charges.

The school's curriculum, liberal by the standards of its day, appeared circumscribed to later generations. The classics and mathematics were at its heart, with courses in the same subjects being listed year after year. These were supplemented, however, by a refreshing infusion of modern languages and history. More important, the teaching was often of a nature to open young minds to vistas beyond the classroom. Lucid and expressive use of the English language was cultivated throughout, and indeed the poems, orations, and essays of students of these middle years are models of their kind.

Competitive sports began to form an important role in student life. Early cricket matches at the school had been in the nature of pageants rather than serious contests. Dr. Coit liked cricket, not because it was an English game, but because it was leisurely and quiet, and it became a regular feature of school holidays. At first, cricket matches were held on the lawn between the School House and the pond. But in 1870 an enterprising student, Richard Henry Dana III, approached Dr. Coit with the idea of clearing land on the far side of the Turkey River, now known as the Lower Grounds. The Rector was skeptical, but conceded that Dana knew more about cricket than he did and eventually gave his permission.

Informal rowing races on the school pond had also begun early, but this sport, too, was set for a major advance. Again, students took the initiative and won out over the Rector's initial reserve. He was ready enough to see the school rowers divided into two clubs, and allowed that to name one of them "Shattuck" was a good way to honor the school's founder.[1] The Rector, however, objected to the idea of having races on Long Pond—what he called "a distant sheet of water, accessible to the public." His hesitations were overcome when he was assured that no public notice or advertisement of the races would be permitted.

On June 7, 1871, the school's first true Race Day took place. Two new four-oared boats had been ordered, but these failed to arrive on time. The old *Ariel*, veteran of encounters on the school pond and recently damaged by vandals, was repaired and put into service. On the day set, under a light rain, a small regatta appeared on Long Pond—several rowing and sail boats along with the steamboat *Penacook* bearing spectators. The Halcyons had the first try; Shattucks followed; and the former were judged to have made the better time. Thus a tradition, long to continue, was established. The participants retired for tea and a concert.

Meanwhile other activities within the school were increasingly lively and productive. To the *Horae Scholasticae* and the

---

1. Apart from this "honor," the founder is remembered at the school only by the recently established "Shattuck Fellows," a designation awarded for outstanding service to the school. Happily, a biography of the founder is now being written by Dr. Douglas Marshall.

Missionary Society (fruits of the school's earliest years) was now added the Library Association, programs related to the school's nearby orphanage (Coit House), and numerous informal contests, exhibitions, clubs, and literary productions. The student was kept more than busy. "Lack of time," asserted a writer in the *Horae,* "is a complaint heard from all sides."

The school would not have been what it was at this period without the presence of some remarkable boys and masters. Among the students, Richard Dana has already been mentioned. Son of Richard Henry Dana, Jr., author of *Two Years Before the Mast,* and grandson of Richard Henry Dana, well-known romantic novelist, the lad's bright and enterprising nature was reinforced by a desire to uphold the family name. He held virtually all the school's important offices, and in one crisis organized single-handed a bucket brigade that saved the old Miller's Cottage from what seemed certain destruction by fire.

Very different was John Jay Chapman, later to become an early leader of civic reform, a battler for human rights, and a noted classical scholar. Chapman was unworldly even beyond anything Dr. Coit wished to inspire—to the point where he was seen kneeling on the cricket field in a state of religious fervor. He left the school in his third year; but he could never put St. Paul's behind him. He became its most eloquent interpreter and its scourge when it departed from what seemed to him its true course.

F. Marion Crawford, who was to be the author of more than forty books and the most widely read novelist of his generation, came to St. Paul's at the age of twelve, already speaking several languages and rich in classical lore. But perhaps the brightest of these special students was Owen Wister. A winning youth, cheerful and self-confident, he showed himself while at St. Paul's to be an accomplished musician, a clever actor, and a fine writer. Among his many later books is *The Virginian,* a novel about the American West, read to this day.

With such students the intellectual life of the school could not be dull. "Those were pleasant times," recalled Hall

The Ariel *on the Lower School Pond.*

The flotilla gathered for the Race Day of 1899.

Star Students
of the 1870s

Richard Henry Dana III

Owen Wister

*John Jay Chapman,
a few years after
leaving St. Paul's.*

Harrison in a letter to Wister, "and I particularly recall how much I enjoyed meeting with you and Chapman three times daily (at least) at the table of the Lower School. Your table talk was, I must say, to me very entertaining...both in its excellent English and its subject matter."

Yet there was a dark side to St. Paul's, as to all educational institutions of this period. Over the civilized and on the whole happy scene hung the cloud of an unrelenting discipline. What a schoolmaster called "the ebullience of schoolboy impetuosity" was highly developed in the early nineteenth century. The English schools, and most public institutions in this country, fell back on corporal punishment. Dr. Keate, the headmaster of Eton, was said to flog everyone for even the most minor offenses, and on one occasion (being nearsighted as well as impulsive) flogged the members of a class that had been brought to him for Confirmation. The great Dr. Arnold, a wit remarked, ruled Rugby as if it were a remote province constantly on the point of mutiny.

At St. Paul's neither corporal punishment, nor the conduct that might have tempted its use, was common. But constant supervision combined with a network of regulations harassed the students. From waking to sleep their conduct was determined by the clangor of bells; they were watched closely in class and outside. Marks in punctuality, industry, and decorum supplemented the academic ratings which the Rector read out every Saturday afternoon for every boy in the school, from the second to the sixth form. In addition, after chapel each morning the Rector would intone the list of offenders of the day and declare the punishments meted out to them.

Chief form of punishment was the writing of "sheets"—the copying out, over and over, of a selection of Latin lines. The practice was despised by the students, not only because of its tedium and humiliation, but because it encroached on their free afternoon hours. The more clever found ways to circumvent, or at least to abbreviate, this form of mental torture. Binding several pens together, they devised an early form of copying machine. Others would accept the alternative of corporal punishment.

The Horae *board of 1877: Owen Wister, seated, at left.*

For those who were consistently lazy or unruly, the last re-sort was expulsion. The Rector would send boys home, but al-ways reluctantly, and with the uncomfortable feeling that somehow he had failed as schoolmaster and as pastor. To ban-ish young men from the Eden he had created was too much like an act of God, which even he did not relish undertaking. Actually, the school records show nothing in the way of rebel-lious or shocking acts. If young men dreamed of tripping up the Rector or escaping to a larger world, they apparently never put such dreams into effect. Discipline was more than anything a way of keeping everyone on his toes. However galling it may have appeared at the time, it seems to have been accepted as part of a paternalistic society—an aspect of family life that was to be borne with patience.

4

A Troubled Year

1878

A turning point in the school's life may be said to have occurred in the academic year 1877–1878, twenty-one years after the founding. Dr. Coit had always worried about whether the school would endure. The examples of Round Hill, of Flushing Institute, and of St. James College were constantly in his mind; St. Paul's, like them, could prove a short-lived dream. "Hitherto hath the Lord helped us," Dr. Coit declared on the school's twenty-fifth anniversary. Would He continue to do so in the future?

Dr. Coit was perhaps beginning to feel the first lessening of the energy that had carried him so triumphantly through the early years. Moreover, finances were becoming a problem. Until the mid-seventies he was able to make receipts balance expenditures. Now the expenses of several new buildings—a new study hall, a new building to house the upper school—were beginning to be felt. A request to Dr. Shattuck resulted in a loan, which the Rector soon repaid. Subsequently Dr. Shattuck wrote to the Board pointing to the need for a financial underpinning which would, among other things, provide a salary for the Rector. With the letter went his own gift of $3,000—a considerable gift in today's dollars.

The Board consisted mostly of friends of Dr. Shattuck and had formed the habit of injecting themselves as little as possible into the school's affairs. Their duties were minimal; their terms were for life, and several were absent over long periods. Among Board members were Richard H. Dana (whose son we

Samuel Eliot—orator on great occasions.

have already met); Samuel Eliot, a distinguished orator who adorned with his eloquence significant school occasions; Edwin Newton Perkins, Jr., of Jamaica Plain, remembered mostly for his puns; and his relative, Charles Perkins Gardiner, of Brookline, with a fine taste in the arts and architecture. In 1879 Henry Ferguson, clergyman and professor of history at Trinity College, Hartford, Connecticut, became the first graduate of the school to be elected to the Board.

To these men with their varied gifts the financial stability of the school was now entrusted.

More serious than a vague worry about money matters was constant concern for the health of the students. Diseases of the young struck swiftly in those days, and frequently with mortal effects. Pneumonia, scarlet fever, and diphtheria were constantly feared, and even measles could be a cause of deep anxiety. Between 1871 and 1875 several deaths occurred among the students. "We greatly need a proper infirmary, or sanatorium, for our sick boys," Dr. Coit wrote to friends of the school, adding the hope that he would not be thought presumptuous for thus calling attention to the most urgent of the school's needs.

Samuel Eliot took charge of a fund-raising campaign; the necessary $6,000 was quickly raised, and by the close of 1876 a simple frame building, next to the new rectory, opened its doors.

In 1878, illness struck again. An epidemic of scarlet fever broke out, and in November the school was hastily dismissed. Physically and emotionally exhausted, Dr. Coit expressed his hope that the boys, "with their good and gentle ways," would be more than ever welcome at their homes.

The school's new Infirmary, situated next to the Rectory (it later became the dormitory known as "Twenty House").

Reopening for the winter term, the school found itself in the grip of new disasters. By the end of February forty-five boys were confined with measles. As if fate were showing that illness fell on the favored and unfavored alike, all but two of the boys in the school's nearby orphanage were stricken. Two St. Paul's students perished of sudden, unrelated illnesses; by early spring death had claimed two more by scarlet fever.

Nevertheless amid that winter's gloom, there occurred an interlude bright with joyousness and laughter, a reaffirmation of youth's undying spirit. For Washington's Birthday Mrs. Coit invited two young women, Emily Eliot, daughter of Samuel Eliot, with Mary Brown, a niece of Mrs. Shattuck, to make "a little visit" to the school. The girls were thrilled at the prospect of being amid

Emily Eliot, 1878—
a welcome visitor.

The Rectory as it appeared in the Coits's day.

so many young men, and were not at all disheartened when a heavy snowfall gave Mrs. Coit an excuse to extend their visit. They sleighed, coasted; attended a meeting of the Missionary Society (where the treasurer's problems with mathematics amused them no end); were serenaded in an impromptu concert; and watched a play of which Owen Wister was the author and star.

For five days these two vivacious and coquettish young women charmed the school. They were not awed by Dr. Coit and saw through the pretensions of certain members of the faculty. When they left, escorts accompanied them to the station in their sleigh and others rode behind with the team carrying their trunks. In the railroad car all sang *Salve Mater*, and the more enthusiastic followed the train on foot as it departed.

"So ended," wrote Emily in her diary, "a delightful, unique

The old "Mother House," before the fire of 1878.

experience and one never to be forgotten." They could not have known that some ninety years later girls would arrive to live at St. Paul's, not as visitors, but as full participants in its life.

The girls had watched as Owen Wister, suddenly struck by the measles, was carried into the infirmary "in a very corpse-like way." He was being joined hourly by others, yet the young visitors seemed to have no inkling of how grave a crisis was developing.

The Rector, who had appeared to the girls "very pleasant and kind," was actually in a state of growing alarm. As the epidemic spread, he gave parents the option of bringing their sons home, and in May declared the term at an end. In a moving letter he referred to "the great shock and strain" to which he and others at the school had been subjected, and thanked the boys for their loving and cordial support "in this great trouble."

The time of trouble was not, however, at an end. In July of that summer, in the midst of heat and drought, sudden lightning struck the old School House and reduced it in a few hours to a smoking ruin.[1] This was the building in which the school had begun, the "mother house" which, with many alterations and additions, still lodged many of the school's activities.

In vain the school bell sounded across the countryside; neighbors thought it was summoning them to church, and as one of them said afterwards, "I wasn't calculating to go." A messenger on horseback went out to summon the Concord fire department, while farmhands and a few members of the staff fought ineffectually against the flames.

Dr. Coit, on a trip to Newfoundland, received a telegram en route. He returned to Concord by the earliest train, to face the destruction of much he had been building for twenty years.

---

1. One object miraculously saved from the fire was a round rosewood table originally bought in France by Dr. Shattuck and used in the dining room of his summer home. Around this table the Trustees of the school first met and here Dr. Shattuck signed the deed of gift of his property. In recent years the table was rediscovered in a school barn. Restored, it now stands under the central dome of Sheldon.

5

The Kings Depart

1880–1891

As a result of extraordinary exertions the school reopened on time for the autumn term of 1878. Accommodations for eighty boys had been contained in the School House. These were now provided by building a new cottage; by adding a second floor to the old Miller's Cottage, and by adapting a ward in the infirmary for dormitory use. A new dining room and kitchen were constructed. When the autumn term opened, 204 boys were in residence, compared with 194 the previous year.

The school had emerged successfully from its year of sickness and destruction. But in many ways things were never to be the same again. The world was changing rapidly, and within the school a generation which had been responsible for so much of its unique character was beginning to lose force. The decade of the 1880s was looming ahead, its emphasis on wealth and materialism fitting ill with the ideals which Henry Coit strove to impart.

For the Northern states, the trauma of the Civil War was over; new industrialists were coming to power, driven by new ideas. The rich and the very rich were sending their sons to St. Paul's, not because it was an idyllic country school, but because its mixture of discipline, high educational standards, and energetic Christianity offered a pathway to worldly success. On the school's lists appeared such names as Vanderbilt, Mellon, Morgan. Private railway cars could be seen waiting in the

Concord station, and the sons of at least one such family were segregated in a master's house rather than being subjected to the rough amenities of dormitory life.

Dr. Coit was not greatly impressed by wealth; he could treat with rather offhand courtesy such plutocrats as passed his way. Their offspring he accepted as part of the varied crop of humankind. Educating them was not less important than educating the poor, to be undertaken with persistence and pious hope. If the coming of the new age meant anything to Coit and to his little band of the faithful in Millville, it meant a more determined withdrawal into their own dream. Concord's distance from such

A "snap-shot" of Dr. Coit in his hey day.

The Old Chapel, center of an intense religious life.

centers of financial power as Boston and New York, its existence amid what writers of that day liked to call "the bleak
New Hampshire hills," strengthened the faithful in their withdrawal, while it convinced the wealthy that their sons were
being made vigorous and independent.

The decision to build a new and larger chapel was an outward symbol of the school's rejection of many of the values of the
time. St. Paul's did not really need a new chapel, and when plans
for it were first broached, they were opposed by many alumni.
The Old Chapel, moreover, perfectly suited Henry Coit's style of
preaching and his ideals of religious ritual. Here for more than a
quarter century he had impressed his faith and his personality on

the Millville community. His presence seemed to fill the place as his words permeated and controlled the congregation. The New Chapel was never to be the same for him.

The committee of alumni which undertook to launch the chapel drive announced the altogether unheard-of goal of $100,000. The school had recently completed a new study hall, paid for largely by borrowing. Besides, a general need for better maintenance was becoming apparent, and the school had no endowment. Nevertheless the drive went forward, at first with disappointing results. Two years after the first appeal a third of the necessary sums were still lacking, and even the boys of the school were called on to help.

Slowly the required amount accumulated, until on April 3, 1886—just thirty years after the first day of the school—Coit received word from the alumni that the chapel building fund had reached its goal.

Designed by a young English architect, Henry Vaughan, the Chapel was dedicated June 5, 1888. Present for the occasion was the largest number of alumni that had ever returned to the school at one time. The structure was incomplete. What was to be its tower was a truncated section rising just above the roof of the nave. Windows were bare of stained glass, while the altar, the pulpit, and many other interior details were in improvised form. Yet the building of dark brick stood imposingly, set back from the Millville street, and the richly carved stalls waited to receive students and masters not only of that day, but of generations to come.

This should have been a time of unrelieved rejoicing for the school. In fact it was shadowed by illness and impending death. The previous winter the Rector had fallen on the ice and broken his leg. Thereafter he was a crippled man. His wife Mary was suffering from an incurable disease and died the following summer. The indispensable support of Henry Coit, she had been since the school's first day a presence of concern and cheer. She kept an eye on the boys in sickness and health; and she had, as a friend recalled, "the brightness of mind that gave her insight into their peculiarities."

Further losses were to come. In 1893 Dr. Shattuck died. "A prince has fallen," wrote the keeper of the school journal. Indeed, no founder could have played his role with more magnanimity or more tact. Careful never to interfere, he was an unfailing source of professional as well as financial help. In good times and bad he was a robust, invigorating person. "To think of him," wrote Samuel Eliot, his peer, "was to be a part of bright scenes, vivid converse, hearty merriment....His presence was a gift over and above all his other gifts."

Dr. Coit carried on his schedule unremittingly through years when his strength and spirits were declining. He was not at home in the new age of materialism, as he was never really at home in the unfamiliar and still-unwarmed spaces of the New Chapel. Yet he awoke at earliest dawn, and before the rising bell he was at his desk, carrying on without secretarial assistance an immense correspondence with alumni and with parents of boys and of prospective students. Through the door of his study, which was open to all comers, he could be seen scratching away with a quill pen, or perhaps sitting by the radiator on a low rocking chair, poring over a book of sermons. After an early lunch he would frequently be driven to Concord, where he distributed provisions to the aged and infirm of his extended school parish. If a cricket match was being held, his returning carriage would pause briefly at the Lower Grounds.

Increasingly, in this period, Dr. Coit depended for the running of the school upon members of his family. His brother, Joseph Coit, had long been the sage vice rector. His son Charles returned, briefly and reluctantly: it had been difficult being a student at the school under so dominant a father, and to be a master revived painful memories. A different case was that of the Rector's second son, Joseph H. Coit II, who was known as "Bull" and in his robust insensitivity lived up to the name. Finally, the Rector's younger brother, Milnor. He had

The New Chapel, its tower still uncompleted.

come to the school amid the troubles of 1878 and served faithfully in the new infirmary. But he was unlike the Rector, at whose side he was now constantly to be seen—a hearty man whom nobody quite trusted.

The school went forward, in all essential things upon a smooth course. Students had their days of misery and happiness; they learned and resisted learning; and when they graduated, they went forth as alumni remembering the old place and serving it according to their gifts. The traditions and the institutions persisted. All that was missing was the vital élan—the creative impulse in boys and masters that had been responsible for the accomplishments of the last two decades. How much that impulse was dependent on the Rector was evident, now that his leadership had begun to wane.

The New Chapel interior, giving a sense of lightness and height.

The night of February 4, 1895, was particularly severe, even by Concord's standards. The thermometer sank to sixteen degrees below zero and the winds were rising. Oblivious of the weather two of the school's masters—John Hargate and James Potter Conover (the Rector's son-in-law)—could have been observed outside the Rectory door: "just waiting," as one of them later recorded; "waiting in perfect silence with no account of time." These two were keeping the last watch, as Henry Coit's life ebbed away.

In the Big Study next morning Joseph Coit announced the Rector's death. His body was moved across the street to rest in the Chapel, where boys and masters attended it through the night. The day of the funeral saw a fierce snowstorm in Millville, so that many old boys were prevented from returning and students were kept from taking part in the procession. Those who gathered at the graveside never forgot the wild howling of the tempest.

Dr. Coit left an image larger than life. "To have known him," wrote John Jay Chapman, "is to have come into contact with all the piety, the romanticism, the mystery...which flamed over Europe in medieval times." He was the seer, the prophet, the predestinate founder; and in his later years, goading and guarding the thing he made, he had become something of a tyrant. Yet many remembered the earlier Coit, "the poet, the dreamer," in words of Owen Wister; "the delicate scholar and discerning critic," who so often won over the boy in trouble and left with even the most worldly a sense of other worlds than their own. Now he was gone, and the school gathered its forces to face a new day in which its ideals and its very existence would be at stake.

6

St. Paul's in Babylon

1895–1906

In June 1895, the Trustees formally elected Joseph H. Coit the second rector of St. Paul's. It was an easy, indeed an inevitable, choice. Moreover, in almost all respects it was a good one. An adverse factor was Coit's age—at sixty-four he was already five years older than the brother he succeeded. He was also deeply identified with the old regime—at a time when fresh leadership was urgently called for.

The handicap of age was insurmountable. The second half of his eleven-year term saw Coit sink into senility, becoming a tragic caricature of the large-minded man known to generations of students. Yet at the start of his term he was remarkably successful in escaping from the shadow of his brother and providing a needed program of reform.

For Joseph Coit the system of discipline in his brother's last years must have tried even his unwavering loyalty. Rules of student conduct had congealed into a complex series of restrictions, punishments, and banishments, with the right of appeal narrow at best. The Sunday schedule with its three obligatory chapel services and its ban on most leisure activities was archaic. The new rector moved to introduce a more humane and flexible regime, in keeping with his own genial nature.

He also introduced academic reforms. The masters of that period had come to play the role of autonomous chieftains, fixing the content of their courses and setting their own examinations.

Coit appointed responsible department heads. He mitigated the predominance on the faculty of alumni masters, often eccentric and financially well off, bringing in a group of highly professional teachers, several of whom would serve into the 1930s.

Nor did the financial problems of the school escape him. Henry Coit had kept tuition unreasonably low, while relying on appeals to wealthy benefactors among his friends. In 1896 his successor placed before the Board the urgent need for a permanent endowment. An appeal was launched, and if at first it was not notably successful, it set the course for what in the future would become one of St. Paul's greatest strengths.

Joseph II. Coit, the second Rector.

On the terrace of the new Sheldon Library, unveiling at Anniversary, 1906, of the Spanish-American War Memorial.

The school grounds received many new buildings. Under Joseph Coit the old Lower School was completely remodeled, to survive for many decades as the "Middle." (A new Lower School had been erected in Henry Coit's last years.) The "Upper" that still stands grandly and rather isolated upon its hill was constructed, a building at various times loved and derided. More serious than architectural flaws was the sense of exclusivity it imparted to its residents. Much of the trouble in the school from the time of its completion in 1904 through the 1920s originated here.

Finally, in 1901 a new library, given by the family of William C. Sheldon in his memory, was dedicated. It was placed on the site of the famous Miller's Cottage, an impressive gray granite building designed by Ernest Flagg with red tile roof, its pediment crowned by large granite globes. Hailed by the students as "the Taj Mahal of the Western hemisphere," it survived (shorn of its red tile roof) as the school library until 1990. Today the building, splendidly restored, has been put to other uses.

Athletics were becoming an increasingly important element of school life. From the informal scrimmaging of the 1860s they had developed into the pageantry of the next two decades. Now they were highly organized and competitive. Boxing and tug-of-war were briefly popular. Racquets, or squash, had been played at least since 1882, when the first racquet courts in the country were built at St. Paul's. In the 1890s the game was avidly pursued. But now football became the focus of SPS athletics, with

A new enthusiasm for sports—the SPS football team of 1895.

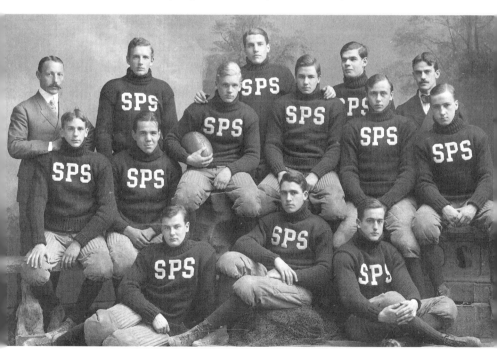

The Lower School Pond with its nine hockey rinks.

the school divided into three clubs, Delphians, Old Hundreds, and Isthmians.[1] The heroes of the Lower Grounds soon looked for wider fields of conquest, and in 1895 we find a St. Paul's team pitted against Harvard seniors. (The St. Paul's team lost.) A few years later a professional fresh from gridiron victories at Yale was brought in to coach the SPS team.

Hockey, meanwhile, was taking on something of its present form. In the mid-1890s the Canadian version of the game was introduced into the United States, and the school played its first game, against a team of alumni, on the fabled St. Nicholas rink in New York. The encounter was a spectacular event, and St. Paul's was off upon a long career of hockey playing. The skills of its players were to make St. Paul's known in the sports world and to fill many of the top college teams with skaters trained upon Millville's ice.

The gentlemanly game of cricket began to fade out, supplanted by the more competitive and more American game of baseball. In the late 1880s the Rector forbade baseball, but the decision was widely unpopular, and for once his will failed to carry. The growth

1. Henry Kittredge, the sixth rector, liked to tell the story of the first former who wrote to his father that he was a "Simian." The father replied that he had always suspected as much.

of baseball was an indication that in the new world St. Paul's was entering, even Coit could not keep an absolute control.

In other fields than athletics, the St. Paul's students were beginning to feel themselves a part of the contemporary world. They might still wear the traditional narrow, pointed shoes, stiff collars, and scratchy woolen underwear; yet beards and sideburns were sported, inconceivable to an earlier generation. They still asked formal permission before going for a walk or into town. Yet smoking and drinking were common, not only among sixth formers but throughout much of the school.

Concord was getting very up-to-date.

Relations between masters and boys, once so familiar and trusting, deteriorated. Students would "pick on" hapless newcomers to the faculty, hoping to ensure for them a brief stay. Classrooms were often disorderly; one can almost hear across the gap of time the crash of books thrown at the heads of offending students, or the sound of masters yelling their instructions. The alumni, up until now an entirely benign force, began to intrude upon the school's affairs, encouraging the students in some of their worst offenses.

A sign of the times was the development of secret societies, imitating those on many college campuses. Occult proceedings, aimed at nothing in particular, extended back into the 1870s, harmless outgrowths which Henry Coit would have done well to

The road through the school, c. 1890.

stifle at birth. Now they became part of the incipient disorder of the time, sources of schoolboy intrigues or (more ominously) of plots against hapless masters.

In the midst of all this, Joseph Coit's health began to fail. After 1902 he was increasingly absent from the school; when in residence he was rarely seen. Groping slowly for words, dozing off in the midst of interviews, in chapel his voice sounding thin and weak, he was a pathetic residue of a once worldly and benevolent man. Masters at the school made no allowances for an illness that could not be diagnosed, while students took fiendish advantage of his lapses.

Undeclared war between masters and students led to excesses on both sides. In Big Study, when a master rang the bell for silence, he was greeted by jeers and catcalls that could be heard on the Lower Grounds. In the dormitories and dining halls even long-respected members of the faculty were derided, looked on—as an old boy remembered—as "a necessary evil, who spied on us from behind closed doors, who trailed us when we went off into the woods, who tore down our huts."

Masters responded not only by venting their anger—occasionally in physical assaults, more regularly by slipping away on absences that saw them return to school the worse for wear. A few faculty consoled themselves by adopting standards of high living, new to Millville. Milnor Coit, wrapped in furs that made him look like a Russian grand duke, drove a painted sleigh drawn by fast horses. The roasts and other rich food with which the school stocked his house seemed excessive even for one of so solid a figure. Other members of the school community built up large charge accounts in Concord, some of them remaining unpaid into the twentieth century.

Still Joseph Coit clung to his post.

In January 1896, John Hargate died at the school. He was a beloved figure; he had been like a son to Henry Coit, and his passing was seen as the passing of a bright and fondly remembered age. From the South a short while later came word that

Joseph Coit was sinking. In March of that year he died, far off and unregretted, having outlived the memory of his ability and charm.

The year was 1906, and at Anniversary that June the fiftieth year of the school's existence was marked. It could hardly have fallen at a less propitious time. In addition to the sobering cloud of recent deaths, the weather was dark and rainy, and the future looked gloomy indeed. The *Horae* struck the one cheerful note, remarking on the unusually large number of girls attending the sixth form dance. "Hitherto there has been a scarcity of the gentler sex, but this time it was different, and no one who attended ever had much spare time on his hands."

There would come a time when the "gentler sex" was permanently in evidence in Millville. But before that a new leader, as strong, and in the end as creative, as the first Coit, would come onto the stage and restore the school's fortunes.

Trained on Millville's ice—the famous hockey player Hobey Baker with Willard Scudder, master.

PART TWO

7

On a New Path

1906–1910

During Joseph Coit's decline the Trustees had taken the step of electing a new rector, to succeed to the post in due course. Their first choice was a young clergyman, Anson Phelps Stokes, Jr., destined for a brilliant career in the church. He declined, and the Trustees then turned to one of their own—an "old boy" and a member of the Board.

In 1906 Henry Ferguson was an amiable and heart-warming man. In his youth he had participated in an extraordinary adventure which made him famous. Not yet twenty, he embarked with his older brother on a clipper ship for a voyage around the Horn. This had for its purpose—ironically as it turned out—the restoration of the latter's precarious health. Having rounded the Horn, on a windless sea and under a burning sky the ship caught fire and was totally consumed. Two lifeboats put forth, lashed together. One presently broke loose and was lost. The other, including in its crew Henry Ferguson and his brother, continued on a voyage which remains to this day a classic example of endurance at sea.

In an open boat, minimally provisioned, fifteen men traveled for forty-three days across three thousand miles of the Pacific. They landed, when all hope seemed gone, on a South Sea island. Amid threats of mutiny and cannibalism, Henry Ferguson had played a key role in bringing the boat to safety. Preparation of this sort was unusual for a future rector of St. Paul's!

After the long sea voyage: Henry Ferguson, center, with his brother and the captain of the ill-fated ship. In Honolulu, 1866.

Something of the aura he wore after this long sea voyage of his youth, a quiet self-mastery and easy sense of command, remained below the surface of a charmed and happy life. Married to a woman of wealth and social position, he moved in intellectual circles at Trinity, among old friends and in elegant surroundings. From all this he tore himself away, reluctantly and at the insistence of the Board, to take up the reins at Concord.

On his arrival at the school, Ferguson found all in disorder. The bonds that had held the little community together were worn threadbare, and the physical plant was in decay. Ferguson's practical bent led him to deal first with the physical environment. The power plant was being mismanaged; the school farm could not even supply enough potatoes for the boys; the Chapel and classrooms were shabby and ill-ventilated. Ferguson confessed that he had the greatest difficulty in controlling his drowsiness during chapel services—and the boys, he added charitably, "are frequently absolutely unable to do so."

Accompanying all this was a method of bookkeeping primitive to say the least. The first Coit had been in the habit of simply pocketing funds as they came in and disbursing them as needed. As the size and complexity of the school increased (and as the sense of responsibility weakened), it became impossible to control expenses or to trace fees and contributions.

These problems were bad enough; more vexing to the new Rector was dealing with older, conservative masters.

When he fired the manager of the power plant (a master with roots in the old regime), the alumni banded together in protest. Milnor Coit, brother of the first Coit, conspired to stir up this mischief. Continuing in the post of vice rector, he was a focus, as well, of controversy within the school. Ferguson could not easily force his retirement, nor was he entirely confident that he could run the place without him.

A second holdover, the first rector's younger son, Joseph H. Coit, Jr., kept a seat of power as head of the Upper. He felt the chill of a fresh wind blowing; but unfortunately he had built up debts to the school, for vast quantities of firewood, eggs, milk, and blacksmith services. In such circumstances it was difficult to oust him.

Ferguson negotiated the departure of these men, and then turned to the problems of the boys. He never really understood boys, but he cared for them and respected them, and at the end he could justifiably express the modest hope that what he had done or left undone had been of no injury to any of them. In dealing with them he saw as paramount the twin issues of discipline and scholarship.

It was not to be supposed that the unruly habits of the past decade would immediately cease. Indeed the students, having "sworn off" smoking when the new Rector arrived, were soon unrepentantly back at the old vice. The Rector, nevertheless, added a carrot to the punitive measures then in force. Believing the worst of boys to be capable of reform, or at least subject to temporary remissions, he made it possible for them to work off by good behavior the demerits that had been accumulated by bad. The student body seemed pleased; at least at that year's end the Rector commended them for their "good spirit" and their "cheerful good behavior."

The drive to enter college was now universal, success being determined by competitive examinations. In these, St. Paul's students were simply not holding their own. Parents and alumni were dissatisfied; the Rector was frustrated. "At examination time," wrote Ferguson, "parents blame us for their sons' inattention and idleness, which we have been struggling to overcome throughout the year." He introduced changes in the curriculum, liberalizing the old core courses, but in the end he was left to console himself with bemused reflection. "I suppose there will never be a time when all boys will be diligent and studious continuously," he wrote in a final report. "The unwillingness of the simple to receive instruction is a complaint as old as the Hebrew sages."

Ferguson had consented to serve for five years only; it was urgent that his successor be named. In 1907 the Trustees elected Frederick J. Kinsman for the post, with the understanding that he would serve as vice rector in the interim. It was a strange choice. A former student and a master for two brief terms, he was an eccentric, unstable man, and his withdrawal was no loss. But this did not occur before another fracas. Joseph Coit II, in his last days at the school, was opposed to Kinsman on personal

Henry Ferguson as Rector.

grounds, and came close to getting the standing committee of the Alumni Association to condemn the Trustees' action. The dangerously divisive vote was fortunately avoided at the last minute.

Thereafter Ferguson undertook to find his own successor, and this in the end, despite all his other contributions to the school, was perhaps his greatest. In the Philippines at that time, in the burgeoning city of Manila, a young missionary, Samuel S. Drury, was waiting out the weeks until his eight Igorot pupils should gather at their new schoolhouse in the north. The renowned Bishop Charles Brent of Western New York heard the young man preach in the cathedral, and afterwards had a talk with him.

With his Igorot students, Samuel S. Drury as a missionary in the Phillipines, 1906.

"He was very reserved—which I like," wrote Drury to his mother; "I mean to be so myself." He added nonchalantly that the Bishop hoped he (Drury) would one day be elected rector of St. Paul's School in Concord.

This prophetic hint required several seasons and strange shifts of fortune before it was to be realized. After a year in the Philippines—a decisive year in his development—Drury returned to his native Rhode Island. Meanwhile Bishop Brent had evidently commended him to Henry Ferguson as a possible master at the School. In the autumn of his return, Drury was surprisingly and unexpectedly called to be rector of Boston's St. Stephen's Church. He received at about the same time a letter from Ferguson inviting him to come to the school and preach.

St. Stephen's in 1908 was an unusual church. Founded by Phillips Brooks, it served a large congregation, mostly the poor of Boston's South End, who came not only for spiritual comfort but for the social services embodied in health services, a gymnasium, a library, and classes in almost everything from dancing to carpentry. For a young man still at the threshold of ordination the call was an extraordinary one, and after some weeks of doubt and self-doubt Drury accepted. Less than a week later he made his first visit to Concord.

A less patient man than Ferguson might have considered the matter of the St. Paul's rectorship closed. But after the visit he went down to Boston to have a long talk with Drury. The younger man declared himself bound to St. Stephen's. The declination still did not convince Ferguson, and over the next year a tactful and delicate exchange of letters, and two further visits to the School, took place. Meanwhile Drury was making a deepening impression in his new post, not only on his parishioners but on others drawn by the spreading word of his preaching. Yet in spite of this success—or perhaps because of it—Drury heeded the unanimous call of the St. Paul's School Trustees, agreeing in the autumn of 1909 to become Rector, after a year in residence as vice rector.

Bishop Brent deserves the last word in this affair. "Rejoice," he wrote to the young man whom he had promoted, inspired, cajoled; "Rejoice that God has given you such a wonderful work to do for mankind. You are favored as only one man in a generation is favored. Again, I say rejoice!"

8

Drury Takes Command

1910–1919

In the autumn of 1911, after a frustrating year as second in
command, Samuel Drury, aged thirty-two, moved with his
bride into the Rectory. He had met Cornelia Woolcott as a volunteer worker at St. Stephen's. She was of a wealthy and socially
prominent family, the daughter of a Massachusetts governor, and
their marriage that previous spring had been an event of the
Boston season. The Rectory, dull gray until then, had been
painted a gleaming white for their coming, and was bright with
newly installed electricity. Drury—Dr. Drury as he would always
be known thereafter—lost no time in getting down to work.

His first report to the Trustees, submitted early in the autumn, was composed in what he termed "a conservative spirit."
Others, hearing it, may well have judged it differently.
Schoolmastering involved the art of ruling men, Drury began;
modesty might be an innate virtue; but the head of a school
must banish it, steering a course which would often provoke
dissent and the charge of autocracy. The scholarly tone of the
School, he continued, would have to improve notwithstanding
the fact that parents might often set a higher value on varsity
athletics than on a Phi Beta Kappa key. The students of St.
Paul's were not "dumb," but city high schools were "filled with
young people desirous to learn, while our boarding schools fit
their pupils for the pleasurable arts of an idle existence."

Nor did the faculty escape his comment. "We cannot provide the best education," he declared, "from the hands of gentlemanly amateurs."

A first test of Drury's leadership came during the unusually severe winter of 1912. With temperatures dropping as low as thirty-four degrees below zero, the School suffered a record number of severe cases of the grippe. That same winter a lower schooler, Edmund Armour, died of infantile paralysis. Drury resisted, with stinging words, those who wished to close the school before the regular vacation. "Parents who are none too militant about their boy's studies," he said, "become in many instances fearsomely definite when he has the mumps."

The Trustees, in their spring meeting gave "complete assent and approval" to the Rector's actions during this crisis. At the same time they took note of a gift, the largest up to that time in the school's history, of a new infirmary. It was donated by the family of the young victim of that stormy season. Later, in a sermon at Princeton University, Drury recounted some elements of this experience. "Truth sat at the table," he said, "and for once did all the talking." He had indeed been handsomely vindicated, but the conviction that some outside power had directed his moves would return to haunt him, in later decisions leading to less happy results.

Meanwhile the students were forming their own judgment of this powerful figure at the summit of their little commonwealth. They called him "old Drury," and indeed despite his ardent spirit and his long stride, he had the visage of someone born long ago. During the three decades of his reign there would be those who revered him and those who never lost their fear of him. They would recount, half in good-humored amusement and half as a kind of revenge, endless stories of his eccentricities and his sometimes harsh excesses. But for the moment they were pleased by the bright focus he gave to school life. Especially they liked the fact that he was making the Sabbath at St. Paul's, long a gloomy day with almost all diversions forbidden, a time for expeditions, long walks, informal games.

He moved the day's second chapel service, which had fallen like a cloud across the midafternoon, into the evening hours. There, in times to come, with its familiar hymns and prayers and the Rector's inimitable tones rolling down the long boy-bordered aisle, it became a dearly remembered feature of schooldays. With patience Drury sought to make services throughout the week briefer and more accessible to this youthful congregation. His own sermons were lovingly prepared, pruned of ecclesiastical rhetoric, and timed by a vigilant master to ensure that they did not pass the allotted number of minutes.

When it came to discipline, Drury had the counsel and help of G.P. Milne, known as "the Gyp," a master stern, quizzical, but incontestably just. Drury complimented him on his good sense. "What should a Scotchman have if not sense?" Milne replied. The two maintained an affection and deep respect for each other that outlasted many small differences. Milne perfectly complemented Drury's methods. He was a disciplinarian first and last, not a moralist or pastor. He would act with finality on a difficult case, almost without comment. Yet he responded to his chief's confidence in the students' maturity and basic decency. Drury thanked him at the end for his "unique and brotherly helpfulness....It has meant everything to me personally to be by your side."

Drury turned with verve to the problem of low scholastic standards. To older teachers known for their rigor in the classroom he gave his full support. Theophilus Nelson, dry and peremptory in his teaching of mathematics, was singled out for praise. Even Robert Peck, remembered by generations of students as an unremitting pedant, received the Rector's blessing when failures in his Latin courses fell below the 27 per cent rate then prevalent at the School. Drury also sought out new men: Most of the teachers at St. Paul's, he complained, talked too much and too loud; they gave too much emphasis to isolated facts. "We learn a subject," he wrote, "by the slow and arduous

Two of a
New Generation
of Masters

*John Gilbert Winant, future
governor and ambassador.*

Henry C. Kittredge, future Rector.

process of incorporating it into ourselves." Having persuaded the Trustees to raise salaries, he set out to find the men who could approach teaching in this spirit.

There was, for instance, John Richards. Grandson of Julia Ward Howe and son of the well-known writer Laura E. Richards, he taught English as if he were admitting his students to secrets of incalculable worth. There was John Gilbert Winant, a former student whom Drury prevailed upon to return to the school he had loved. Winant was awkward, inarticulate, yet something in this Lincolnian figure exerted a lasting spell over his students. And then there was Henry Kittredge. Son of Harvard's famed Shakespearian scholar George Lyman Kittredge, he was then attracting notice at the Adirondack-Florida School. Henry proved hard to get. He first rejected the St. Paul's offer. Drury was now as patient, and as wily, as Ferguson had been with him. He appealed to the young man's father (without much success); he wrote with a half-feigned resignation to the young man himself: "Do not forget St. Paul's. You and I will probably be in the teaching business for some time. Maybe we shall yet be co-workers."

Co-workers they were indeed destined to become. The free soul of Henry Kittredge never quite allowed itself to stand too close to the older man's searing flame; but together they contributed greatly to the School, and in due course Kittredge became one of Drury's successors.

More difficult than recruiting new members of the faculty was the problem of dealing with older members who did not seem to be pulling their weight. The new Rector defended militantly before the Trustees his right to dismiss inadequate masters. In informing two men that they were not expected to return he had already aroused "unrest and resentment," he admitted. But he could not accept the doctrine that a man was entitled to stay because he was merely doing his duty. Moreover, dismissals "could not be done in town meeting." A school is a very small place, he said, "and schoolmasters are

December 26, 1918. Hobey Baker went out to the field for one last flight.

sentimentalists." It was best that the deed be done by the Rector, "who alone knows all the facts"—and be done without too much talk or explanation.

The critics kept their silence, at least for a while, and America's entrance into the Great War, in 1917, put all such matters into the background.

St. Paul's was not unprepared for the war. Indeed since the opening of the conflict it had watched the defense of freedom with all its latent idealism aroused. From among alumni like Owen Wister and John Jay Chapman came eloquent pleas on behalf of the allied cause. George Williamson, an English citizen, enlisted in the forces of his own country and was the first of forty-eight St. Paul's alumni to give his life. André Champollion, a young painter, went off to fight for the France of his grandfather and was killed on his first day of battle. The United States had scarcely entered the war when two grandsons of the first rector, Henry Augustus Coit II and Richard Steven Conover II, volunteered. They both paid the supreme sacrifice.

One of the last of the St. Paul's School family to give his life was Hobey Baker, symbol of a generation's gallantry. His fame as a hockey player born on Millville's ice, he had become an ace flyer in the war. Shortly after the armistice and when he had already been ordered home, he undertook to test a friend's plane whose engine had proved faulty. Fifteen hundred feet in the air the engine failed. The plane crashed, and Hobey Baker was killed.

At the school—half in fear, half enviously—the boys watched sixth formers departing for war. Under Gerald Chittenden, a master with a clipped moustache and military air, a hundred and fifty students participated in organized drill and complicated military manoeuvres. Twenty acres of school lawns were plowed and planted in answer to wartime food shortages. In the cloister leading to the Chapel the names of alumni in service were inscribed. "Every morning we go trooping through," wrote Drury, "and in Chapel prayers for the safety of our brethren arise with humble and hopeful confidence."

Noting the restlessness of the student body, Drury called, not for more rigid discipline, but for greater freedom and responsibility. "When times are hard and nerves are tense," he wrote sensibly, "a wise method, it would seem to me, is to trust more and expect less."

Drury's faith was rewarded by seeing the establishment of an effective student government. At the same time the secret societies were dissolved. In later years these societies had become less objectionable than amid the disorders of the 1890s; they were under faculty supervision, and drinking at dinners

The Orphans' Home, founded by the first Coit, was being gradually phased out.

away from the school was forbidden. But they remained a divisive influence within the school; and within the sixth form they formed, in the Rector's words, "an inner circle of control; they keep snobbish boys snobbish." It was a sign of the times that Drury was able to inform the Trustees in 1917 that the entire fifth form had resigned from these societies and pledged themselves not to join any others if they should be formed.

In 1917, also, a major fire at Coit House helped mark the close of an era. The "little orphelings" that in the time of Henry Augustus Coit had come shuffling into Chapel to receive largesse from the St. Paul's students were now as much a tale from the past as were other features of the school's life which Drury subtly banished or was in the process of transforming.

9

Schoolmaster as Prophet

1919–1929

❦

Trouble, when it came, was not from the boys but from a group of older and conservative masters. During the war the younger men on whom Drury had counted—men like Richards, Winant, Kittredge—were off on wartime service. Voices that had been subdued as the new rector seemed to carry all before him now rose in an ominous muttering. Drury had seemed a threat to the little circle that found in Millville a secure, tradition-bound social order—a pleasant existence bounded by the golf course south of the School and the agreeable inn (the Alumni House) at its northern entrance. They reacted to the perceived menace by engaging in endless, destructive gossip—spreading their discontent among alumni and parents.

At the head of this coterie were the two Knox brothers, James and Charles. James Knox had come to the school in its first decade. A gifted organist and choirmaster, he was a devotee of the founding rector. Determined that the old ways be preserved, he denounced what he considered the "cavalierish manners" of the young generation, and disliked its mode of dress—"half sweater, half rough-rider." He was ready to ban from the library such novels as *Tom Jones* or such provocative reading as the article on sex in the *Encyclopedia Britannica*. Drury's re-ordering of the Sunday schedule would act as a "dissolvent," he asserted, and would have a tendency "to weaken moral fibre."

Charles Knox, his brother's ally and alter-ego, had been a

Determined that old ways should be preserved—James C. Knox in his later years.

brilliant teacher of the classics in his younger days, but he aged into inflexibility. Not quite equal with these two, but disaffected and gossipy, was Willard Scudder; and a younger recruit, Lloyd Hodgins, who reinforced the intrigues. As the opposition grew in scope and intensity, Drury decided to strike back. He dared not touch the chief protagonists, but he called Hodgins into his study and notified him that his mastership would not be renewed.

The deed, and the abrupt manner of its execution, aroused a furor in Millville. At a masters' meeting a few days afterwards such Drury stalwarts as Richards and Milne signed a statement accusing the Rector of having breached the basic understandings on which masters were hired. Outstanding figures among the

Drury, right, in his study with Vice Rector William H. Foster.

alumni became embroiled. The Trustees, nevertheless, stood firmly behind Drury. They took the unprecedented step of formally expressing to the Knox brothers dismay at their recent conduct. "The freedom with which each [of the Knox brothers] discusses the policies of the Rector and Trustees is damaging to the school," they asserted. "The Trustees believe that in Dr. Drury they have been fortunate enough to secure the very best man in the country. With his policies in all essentials they are in enthusiastic agreement."

His authority thus reinforced, Drury reconstituted his administration, appointing the young Winant to serve beside a much older master, William Foster, as vice rector. He began to speak out on broader issues of the day. Asking how St. Paul's could best serve the country as a whole, it would not be, he said, "wholly in the old way." With the war over, he saw new demands being made upon youth. Would men returning from the trenches be content to find at home a race of leisurely, cleanly youths "with no conception of anything but how to get into college and how to have a good time?" His preaching outside the School and his presence at educational conferences became more frequent.

Drury was out where a rising young man finds his career opening to sudden opportunities. In April 1921 the lightning struck. He was called to the rectorship of Trinity Church in New York, the largest, most prosperous, and most famous Episcopal church in the nation, its charter running back to the seventeenth century and its wealth extending into some of Manhattan's most valuable real estate. Choice of a rector from outside the parish had seemed unlikely, and when Drury's election came unanimously and without controversy, the triumph was complete.

Acceptance of the post was deemed certain. But Drury hesitated. He had been ten years at the School. In one sense, as Bishop Brent advised him, he had rounded out a period and completed a volume. But was his work there really done? "It all comes down to a matter of divine guidance," Drury wrote to a friend. And so the whole school, and many beyond the school, waited. On May 8, in Chapel on Ascension Day, Drury said he had something "very personal" to announce: he had decided to remain at St. Paul's.

What followed was a kind of revelation. This basically shy man—respected, admired, but loved by few—had struck a wholly unexpected chord within the school family. Masters and boys crowded about him after the chapel service, expressing their pleasure and fervently shaking his hand. The next day, when the Rector came into the Big Study to read Reports , a moment of total silence fell on the crowded scene. And then pandemonium broke loose. Cheer after cheer arose as the Rector stood in unaccustomed embarrassment. "It's the best thing that could have happened to the school," wrote one observant stu-

dent in a letter home. It was "wonderful to think of the benefits every possible thing related to the school will receive from
now on."

Outside Millville the news was received with surprise and
praise. Drury's comment—"I felt my work was not done and
that I should stay here to do it"— was said by *The New York
Times* to show a spirit which "every schoolteacher should
honor and which honors every schoolteacher." The press was
anxious for a glimpse of the man who had turned down
worldly honors to continue in an isolated boarding school. A
reporter arriving in Millville was led down "shaded paths by
little rivers" while Drury told of his educational ideals. "That
you should have made an arduous trip to this remote spot on
purpose to see me," said the Rector in his polite farewell, "is
in itself a fact which impresses me."

That year the Anniversary weekend was especially festive.
In the autumn at a New York dinner in his honor, Drury was
flanked by the presidents of leading universities who acknowledged his contributions to secondary education. He was at his
best that evening. He spoke to the audience in quiet tones and
in a personal vein. Nevertheless the headlines next morning
picked up the fact, which he had undoubtedly not let fall by
chance, that 1,700 boys were on the St. Paul's waiting list.

The celebrations passed, but a change had taken place in
the school and in Drury himself. Nothing after Trinity was to
be quite the same as before. The Rector's restless soul saw a
new mandate for reform; the Trustees and the alumni alternately encouraged and drew back from his challenge to make
St. Paul's into a more representative and broadly-based school.
The Rector's annual reports for 1921 and 1922 were phrased
with a new urgency. For St. Paul's, no less than for himself,
there was not to be an "exclusive, ornamental isolation"; the
school must get "mixed up" with the United States. It is folly,
he wrote, "to run a little reform school for the few within the
confines of a free society."

The admissions "waiting list," with sons of alumni entered ritualistically at birth, seemed a snobbish constraint, and Drury urged the completion of a large endowment drive with ample scholarships for students from a wider public. He envisioned going beyond its own constituency by offering ten full scholarships to students from Europe and Asia. "Let us open our door and step forward," he declared, committing St. Paul's to the task of producing "not only good Americans, but good citizens of the world."

The Trustees were still in a post-Trinity mood and backed Drury's proposal at their meeting of October 1923. By spring, however, a different attitude gained force. These were, after all, times of reaction throughout the country. The Wilsonian idealism was discredited; Harding, and then Coolidge, were in the White House. A faction of the Board began asking: "Why foreigners?"—focusing upon this issue all the latent opposition to Drury's other reforms and to the ever more frequent aspersions he cast upon the rich. When a vote was taken, the proposal for scholarships for foreign students was turned down.

At the same meeting a motion condemning Drury's frequent absences from the school was tabled without a vote. The right to be away for preaching engagements, lectures, educational meetings had been one of the conditions Drury had specifically laid down upon his first accepting the rectorship. These journeys, with the opportunities they offered for mental refreshment and new associations, were vital in his view. Now the twin defeats struck deep. To his diary he confided the burning words: "I refuse to be a club steward acting under a directorship of worldlings."

The identity of some of these "wordlings" may be noted. The Board was very differently composed from the often aging individuals that had nodded over their cigars in the Coit era. It was a mixed group, with its share of solid businessmen and a minority of intellectuals. It had also its eccentric, independent characters, some supportive of Drury, some not. All, in

*Frederick Shattuck, the
Founder's son, a lively
presence on the Board.*

one way or another, saw it as their responsibility to guide the
school actively, according to their own lights.

Henry Ferguson became chairman of the Board in 1915;
his tact—and Drury's deep affection for him—averted any of
the tensions which the situation might have provoked.
Ferguson died two years later and was succeeded by Frederick
Shattuck, son of the founder, present on the school's first day.
His colorful wit and robust common sense made him a favorite
with the Rector, but by 1924, when Drury needed him most,
he had passed from the scene. Most of the others were indeed
businessmen, "a strong lot of men to run a bank," John Jay

Chapman described them. But figures like John D. Dickey, Levi H. Greenwood, and "Judge" John McLane of New Hampshire were enlightened men, holding a balance between the old and the new.

The conservative cause was led by two of the more singular characters. John M. Goetchius had retired from business to enjoy a life golfing and yachting and to give himself wholly to leading the SPS alumni. He is to be credited with the raising of funds which for the first time put St. Paul's on a sound financial basis. But the school of his imagination was a place long since passed away. A Philadelphia physician, Charles D. Hart, joined with Goetchius in leading the attack on foreign students and in criticizing the Rector's absences. He was in the habit of making odd gifts to the School—saplings from rare or famous trees, autographs and old photos, a pair of swans, and a shrunken Peruvian head. If he enriched the School, it was without ever really understanding it.

Two outstanding intellectuals were added to the Board, too late to play a part in the crisis of 1922, but sounding a helpful note when things had cooled down. Anson Phelps Stokes, then Canon of the Washington Cathedral, held the Rector's respect to a point allowing him to express frank criticism in private. Samuel Eliot Morison, grandson of the eloquent Samuel Eliot who had been a Trustee under the first Coit and himself already an outstanding historian and professor at Harvard, joined the Board in the later twenties. His astringent comments made him a somewhat uncomfortable colleague, and he resigned after four years.

If there was restlessness within the Board, it was a reflection of what was going on in the country at large. In the wake of immediate postwar idealism had come a period of prosperity, with materialism and self-indulgence prevailing at all levels. The students at St. Paul's watched men only a little older than themselves come back from a war in which they had experienced all aspects of life and were set to enjoy their liberty to the full. A

Samuel Eliot Morison, Trustee, at the desk in Brimmer Street where his grandfather, Samuel Eliot, had also toiled.

slow-burning rebellion, especially among the older boys, provoked new problems. Breaches of discipline appeared no longer a matter of breaking schoolboy rules but of a general corruption in which society as a whole was conniving.

The same academic year that saw Drury's leadership challenged within the Board saw a disciplinary crisis that went to the heart of his authority among the students—and also to the core of his own self-confidence. It began innocently enough. A victory dinner for the victorious Halcyon crew was held at the school's Alumni House on June 19, two days before graduation ceremonies. It was a fine dinner, Scudder noted in his diary; the speeches were witty and the company thoroughly convivial. But afterwards a different form of celebration took place. Retiring to the Upper, sixth formers passed the challenge cup around, drinking liberally and smoking.

Word quickly reached the Rector, who summoned to his study those whom he believed to have been the chief offenders. Among them were the president of the sixth form, the school's outstanding scholar, and star athletes from almost all the teams. In a weird and extraordinary performance the Rector asked all the boys to pray with him, and then to give their word that they had neither drunk nor smoked during the school year, whether on the school grounds or during vacation. There was a dead silence.

"Gentleman," the Rector said, "you shall not receive your diplomas tonight." They all filed out.

Drury's overwrought feelings following his rebuff by the Trustees had created an impossible situation. Many in the school recognized that the year's sixth form had contained undesirable elements, and action taken sooner would have won support. But Drury's delay until the last night of term, his summary decision without evidence of guilt—not least his request for an oath which few could have taken in good conscience—caused an uproar in the school and among alumni.

That summer at Northeast Harbor in Maine, the Rector found himself self-doubting and half repentant. "Give me a right judgment about the boys," read a diary entry. An alumnus, a friend and admirer of his, accosting him on the village street, accused him of having broken the fundamental principles of Anglo-Saxon justice. He may be right, Drury avowed. "I have an increasing disrespect for my own wisdom." In the end, the offending sixth formers were given their diplomas in English (rather than the traditional Latin), and all were admitted to college.

The sense of an insidious corruption continued throughout the next school year. Drury wanted to know why he had not been forewarned of the widespread drinking among students. Moreover, where had the stock of alcoholic beverages been procured? (It must be remembered that this was in the time of national Prohibition.) Had it been stolen from their fathers' homes, or was it brought in by "chauffeurs"? Rumors persisted of mysterious figures glimpsed at the outskirts of the school grounds—"four girls or so at different times, several young men of sinister aspect." These apparitions were not substantiated, but the Rector took steps to re-enforce the security of the school grounds.

Afterwards there would be difficulties and disappointments, but the dark depths of 1923 would not again be plumbed. Over the St. Paul's landscape the sun would shine once more, and Drury would find within himself the resources that helped him balance the role of schoolmaster and pastor; his judgments would become more patient and humane.

Five years after the events related above, one last test of Drury's commitment to St. Paul's would be presented. In May 1929 he was elected bishop coadjutor of Pennsylvania. Turning it down, he suffered none of the pain that had come with the call to Trinity.

On a spring night when the leaves in Millville were just reaching their fullness, when the airs were warm and the lawns clipped and green in readiness for the return of the alumni at Anniversary next day, word came of Drury's having rejected the bishopric. A large group of boys gathered outside the house of one of the masters, where the Rector was known to be dining. They cheered him as he appeared on the verandah and sang "For he's a jolly good fellow." The Chapel bells rang the hour. The Rector stood in silence for quite a while, and then he said, very simply, that he had heard many wonderful things in his life, but never anything so beautiful as the sound of those bells.

That was all. But the moment seemed in retrospect to mark a turning point in the history of St. Paul's. The man who had so often been at odds with himself and with the School thereafter stood at one with his fate. And the school entered a period of material and spiritual growth, with the man and the institution in an almost perfect harmony.

10

Augustan Age

1929–1938

During the 1930s great changes took place in the school's buildings and grounds. The first concern of the Rector and Trustees was to round out the school's acreage and to make it secure against the ever-threatening encroachment of modern traffic. Several hundred acres were purchased to the south and west so that Big and Little Turkey Ponds were incorporated in the School's domain.

Next, the heart of the school needed to be protected. In earlier days it had been a pleasant distraction to hail the few carts and carriages passing down the road through Millville and branching out toward Dunbarton and Hopkinton. But the automobile changed much. With a shrewd eye toward the future, the Trustees, with the cooperation of the Concord authorities, assured a defensible border. The road toward Hopkinton was moved to give the Infirmary and Foster (the home of the former vice rector, now a dormitory) ample breathing space, and to provide a secluded setting for future masters' houses. On the other side of the school a new road was constructed so that Dunbarton traffic could by-pass most of the school grounds.

The historic center of the school thus became an enclave, its once-public street bordered by the two chapels, the Rectory, the Big Study, and the Lower. Drury, who always disliked the automobile, proposed banning all vehicular traffic. As in much else he was ahead of his time. New landscape converted this central area

Drury catches the eye of youth.

into an elm-shaded green, the sidewalks and fence of former times removed, and with brick pathways curving along the narrowed driveway. It provided a stately and serene effect, but there were some who regretted the loss of the country road they had known.

One other improvement in the landscape was dear to Drury's heart. This was a new footpath leading from the Infirmary to the Upper along the shore of the Lower School Pond. Drury, who loved to name things, christened it "The Long Path." It reclaimed land from the pond and called for a pedestrian bridge where this joined with the Library Pond. The result was to open for pedestrian circulation an area of the school grounds that had been obscured by the backs of unattractive and discordant buildings. The Long Path became increasingly used over the years, giving access to later buildings, such as the new Lower (now Kittredge), built in 1969, and Ohrstrom Library in 1991.

All this was merely the infrastucture—the setting of the stage for the major enterprises of the Drury years. Enlargement of the Chapel was among the most important of these. The building had become too small for its daily congregation of boys: many of them sat on what was known as "monkey benches" bordering the pews. Squeaking under the weight of restless lower-formers, these benches impeded the formal procession in which students both entered and left the services. Ralph Adams Cram, foremost interpreter of the Gothic style, proposed cutting the Chapel in two at the choir and moving the altar, along with the recumbent stone figure of Henry Augustus Coit, two bays to the north. This new seating area, aft of the pulpit, quickly became known as "Sleepy Hollow." In addition, an enlarged choir room and a chancel to contain a war memorial were added.

The alumni body responded enthusiastically, and by 1927 the delicate operation was in progress. The school family watched uneasily as the sliced-off part of the structure, seemingly too narrow to hold itself erect, was slid on rails to its new location. The memorial to those who had lost their lives in the Great War was entrusted to the noted American sculptor Daniel

MILLVILLE
New roads
&
buildings
of the
DRURY YEARS
1938

1 Infirmary
2 Enlarged Chapel
3 Lower School Study
4 Drury House
5 Hargate Dining Hall
6 New Dormitories
7 Friendly House
8 Power Plant
9 New School House
10 Community House

The Chapel was cut in two at the choir.

The enlarged Chapel, along the new school drive.

Chester French. His figure of a nude soldier falling into the arms of an attendant angel was the subject of much controversy (the Trustees intervened to see that "a fig leaf or scarf" was added); but with its quiet message of acceptance and repose the sculpture has stood the test of time better than might have been the case with a more militant theme.

Other building projects went on apace. Drury claimed to dislike physical upheavals—a school, he said, should be "the quietest place in the world"—but he enjoyed adding his personal embellishments to each structure. When a new power plant was built, it had a Gothic chimney, now echoed in the Ohrstrom Library, and across its front was emblazoned the fine scriptural injunction, "O Ye Fire and Heat, Praise Ye the Lord." When Hargate, a new dining hall, was built for the middle forms, he insisted on a scale congenial to the youngsters, and created a small apartment for visitors—spry visitors, since it was at the top of a long circular stair—which he christened The Prophet's Chamber.[1]

The old School, with its high garrets and subterranean bathing facilities, was torn down, and in its place (as noted below) a culminating achievement of the Drury years subsequently arose. Next, across the Turkey River as it flows through the school, four new dormitories, identical in plan and formally arranged around a courtyard, gave each third former a room of his own. A relatively minor undertaking, the conversion of the old gas house to a forum for masters' meetings and debating might have concluded the ambitious building program.

But one July day in 1934 there appeared upon the school grounds two unknown persons, one of whom turned out to have attended the school forty years earlier. The other was the father of two former students. They were, in fact, Edward S. Harkness, the philanthropist, who changed the map of both Harvard and Yale, and his architect, James Gamble Rogers. Not long afterwards Harkness agreed to provide a new educa-

---

1. II Kings 4:10—"Let us make a little chamber, and let us set there for him [the prophet] a bed, and a table, and a stool, and a candlestick…"

tional center for St. Paul's, to arise on the old School site.

In this whole building program, in renovations and additions large and small, the alumni played a determining role. The first Coit had formed the habit of welcoming old boys back, but now they were organized as a watchful, imperial force, their chief outposts in Boston, New York, Philadelphia, and Pittsburgh. Yearly, like the potentates they often were, they brought in their tributes to Millville. A leap in the school's endowment, from $1.1 million in 1920 to $3.6 million ten years later, was supplemented by special gifts for physical improvements. Efficiently organized, their banquets in outlying posts of the empire largely attended, they returned at Anniversary to renew contact with their youth and with the beloved place in which it had unfolded.

Drury looked with some uneasiness upon these developments. After one dinner he confided to his diary that his presence was hardly needed if all the alumni were seeking was "a sentimental chat." If, on the other hand, they wanted to be seriously enlightened, he wished they would do the school the honor of "drinking considerably less champagne." In 1921 the office of the school's alumni magazine, *Alumni Horae*, was set up, not in Millville, but in New York. Drury described the publication as one "*supposed* to emanate from the school." "I have strong convictions," he wrote, "about what would constitute a good alumni paper, but I mean to be pliant and reasonable." Most of the time he was.

At the school, meanwhile, a group of strong and often highly individualistic masters were at work. Older men like Beirne Lay, still teaching when he should have been out to pasture, was liked because he was absentminded in so kindly a way. Covering the blackboard with the symbols of an unresolved equation, he would request one of the class to finish it, gently grumbling, "I've forgotten more algebra than you boys will ever learn." Edward Spanhoofd, with a close-cropped white beard and a mind dry and irreligious, would draw young admirers to his rooms in the Big Study, to enjoy the cool play of his wit and to carry away, often in spite of themselves, the memory of some fragmentary verses of Goethe or Heine. "Whoever heard him say anything that was petty?" asked Drury at the end. "All his communications were cosmic and charitable."

Theophilus Nelson was another of the durable crop surviving from the 1890s. In his mathematics classes an insistence on hard work was tempered by a sarcasm often more humorous than wounding. One day in his class, after the bell had summoned all to their seats, one hapless student continued looking out of the window, his chin in his hand. "Come in, dearie," came Nelson's penetrating tones. "If the architect had wanted gargoyles on this building, he would have placed them there."

Judson Howard was of the same generation, teaching Greek and long in charge of The School with its high-ceilinged dormitories and dining hall. Courtly in his younger days, he continued cheerful and devout as he took charge of the new Hargate.

Beach White, a Harvard graduate and an ornithologist, ruled over the Old Upper. His afternoon teas were famous, held in rooms furnished with Moorish pieces and oriental rugs rising crescendo-like to cover chairs and couches and even climbing up the walls. The place was littered with books, papers, and pipes, and the shelves held a finer collection of books on pipes and tobacco than could be found, it was said, in any library. "I never could make head or tail of his mind in the classroom," recalled one student. But removed from his English classes, on bird-watching expeditions or presiding at the tea table, he was a mine of seasoned humor and detached wisdom.

Bridging the old and the new was Willard Scudder. He had outgrown the apprehensions with which he greeted Drury's first years; but he remained an eccentric, presiding over the dilapidated Middle, teaching English literature (as a former student recalled) "by raising his eyebrows." His bachelor quarters formed the gathering place of the school's top athletes and scholars, while he presided over the Halcyon boat club as if its victories and defeats could shake the civilized world. Old boys returned to pay him obeisance, or during vacations received him in their homes as they might the overlord of some remote principality.

With Scudder ensconced in the Middle, Henry Kittredge reigned over the Lower. The Victorian brick building held its own dining room and dormitories, the latter divided into open cubicles under high cavernous ceilings. The cubicles were cramped and lacked privacy; on winter mornings the few central radiators sizzled ineffectually and the showers seemed a dismal mile from the warm bed. But a hundred or more boys twelve to fourteen years old, found here, as one of them attested to later, "a community of unadulterated delight."

Henry and Gertrude ("Patsy") Kittredge seemed ready for anything. When a group of second formers decided to write and to produce *The Last Days of Pompeii*, the Kittredges reacted as if a volcanic eruption was the most common of things to occur under their roof, and stripped their parlor of its velvet curtains to provide the scenery. One day a revolt developed against the frequency with which squash was served. A petition was sent up to the head table. Kittredge read it attentively. Finally, banging solemnly on the table, "Gentlemen," he said,

Dickensian interior of the old Lower School.

Yet it could be a place of delight—first and second formers at bedtime before their alcoves.

"I have received your petition. I regret I can do nothing about it. It is squash that has made New England what it is. Moreover the school has just received, as a gift from a rich alumnus, a dozen carloads of squash."

His younger colleagues delighted in him, and he watched out for their interests. When one of them received an offer from a rival school, Kittredge counseled against too quick a rejection. "Negotiate, delay, get a letter," he advised. "You will then take the letter to the Rector and say, 'Dr. Drury, smell this.' And he will give you a raise."

As a teacher he was unforgettable. He led boys through the

thickets of learning as a genial guide. "Sure," he would say when some uncouth opinion had been expressed—and then with the most delicate elaboration lead the young scholar to a more seemly version of the truth.

Not a many-sided curriculum, but the many-sided teacher, was Kittredge's answer to better secondary education. When Drury sent him out to report on developments elsewhere in progressive education, Kittredge was not impressed. Contrasting St. Paul's with other schools, he reported back to the Rector: "We are far more likely to stroll into the classroom in the same state of mind as a clergyman I once heard preach in North Perry, Maine. He began his sermon thus: 'As I was coming to meeting-house, my friends, I said to myself, "What shall be the subject of my discourse this morning?"'" Kittredge went on to describe how in one of his own classrooms the discussion had gone unexpectedly from battles to plagues, from the power of the Lord to the social effects of unsanitary surroundings.

"For aught I know," Kittredge concluded, "this may be Progressive Education."

Perhaps not surprisingly, in a community where such figures set the tone, sports and extracurricular activities assumed a classic form. The Concordian and Cadmean literary societies conducted debates under strict parliamentary law. Poems, serious and humorous, were read as if a world were listening. The *Horae Scholasticae*, then the only student publication, printed the news of Millville, alongside the literary productions of young scholars, many of whom would later become known. There were also athletic clubs, scientific clubs, a drama club— until students complained of not having enough time. The Rector responded in classic terms. We have always enough time, he declared, to accomplish the things we really want to do. "The most careless fourth former has as much time as Señor Marconi or Dr. Schweitzer."

Athletics in this heyday seemed no longer to be overemphasized, but took their place among other school activities almost as a celebration. Football games against outside schools were abolished in 1932 in favor of club games played over a long season and under expert coaching by the masters. Hockey teams, however, still competed with other schools. Games played annually against college freshman teams in New York's Madison Square Garden gave the Christmas vacation a brilliant start, with the frequent schoolboy victories reported fully in the New York press. Afterwards a tea dance brought out the season's most promising "subdebs."

In the long winters of those days, the pond behind the Big Study contained nine rinks, where the young and less skilled could play on lower club teams while the stars and demigods of

"The sudden thunder of hockey sticks"—SPS plays against Harvard.

the first team "swooped like falcons," as one alumnus remembered the scene, and "clapped together like fighting cocks."
Years after leaving the school he could still feel, see, hear the afternoon events—the swift figures darting over the gray ice, the
crowds bordering the first team rink, the cries, the thunder of
hockey sticks on the breast-high boards as the puck entered the
goal or was stopped in a spectacular save.

Spring found rowers from all the forms pulling at rowing
machines in the dank gymnasium cellar, and then in the cold
misty afternoons getting their first practice on Long Pond. The
ride back to the school was made in trucks and horse-drawn
barges—the rowers warmed by the camaraderie of the hour
and the singing of old Shattuck and Halcyon songs. Race Day
provided the spectacle of sixteen eight-oar crews upon Long
Pond's crystalline waters, in races perfectly timed, and cheered
from shore by the school family, including crowds of alumni
returned for Anniversary. The festivities of the weekend included a track meet and a dance at the Upper School.

*Before venturing onto Long Pond—the Shattuck crew practicing in
the basement of the old gym.*

Rowing in the icy air of early spring.

Drury moved through these scenes as one perfectly at home in a world he had, at least in part, made. The often stormy relations with the Trustees that had characterized his early years subsided into a genial calm. Goetchius and Hart remained on the Board into their advanced age, but were less busy and meddlesome. Reeve Schley, Charles Dickey, Jr., and later Henry Laughlin were of the post-Coit era, cheerfully accommodating themselves to the changed times. Scholarships were voted for English boys (if not for the Asians Drury had hoped to see at the school). In the matter of absences, which had been so bitter a bone of contention, the Trustees urged Drury to feel free in exercising his own judgment.

A change had come over Drury, too. After rejection of the Pennsylvania bishopric, he looked more warmly upon the school. In matters of discipline he seemed at once more wily and more compassionate. A year after the mass firings from the form of 1923, he faced another potential crisis. This time he warned the rebellious faction in advance, making plain they

Race Day—a victorious Halcyon crew coming down the school street.

would be dismissed if they did not mend their ways. "Actually he was right, we were a bad lot," acknowledged one of them later. Drury's subsequent behavior startled them. He invited them into the Rectory for a succession of Sunday evenings, where he served his own brand of Welsh rarebit and read passages from *Pilgrim's Progress*. There would be also a blazing fire and talk about books, illustrated with volumes from the Rector's abundant library. No sudden firings took place that year—nor afterward.

The Great Depression of the thirties deepened, and St. Paul's adapted to it in its own ways. Workers, normally laid off in winter, were kept on the job clearing the woods. Emergency scholarships were granted discreetly. As gifts fell off and building projects lagged, Drury set about devising small improvements. The bells in the Old Chapel sent forth "an unmelodious summons." Could they not be improved? Could not the electric bells in the Upper School be silenced altogether? He dreamed of a natural swimming pool carved from an unused quarry near the school; he urged a committee of boys and masters especially charged with the look of things—the paths, the gardens, the plantings.

The one big piece of construction to go forward through economic adversity was the new Schoolhouse financed by Harkness. Drury entered into its planning with zest, conceiving it as an opportunity to enhance the whole nature of teaching and learning at the School. He wanted classrooms shaped to small groups of students placed in close relationship with the master, with books upon ample shelves and, where possible, an

Flagpole ceremony at the close of Race Day. A winning oar is raised.

Cornelia and Samuel Drury, on the Chapel steps toward the end of a long reign.

open hearth—an environment suited to hard but leisurely work. Large reading-rooms, spacious quarters where masters could meet for discussion or to be alone, were also part of his plans. Finally, there were exact specifications for the Rector's own study, a small room in comparison to the rest, with direct access to the milling students outside.

All this was largely accomplished within the building's handsome Gothic exterior. It was a building, Drury said, "that we ought to enter with trumpets and banners of high resolve." But when it came time to take up his place in his new study, he was loath to go. In his old quarters, in the crowded little study with its rolltop desk and window seat deep in papers, with its collection of framed photographs and architects' drawings and flourishing green plants, he had for a quarter of a century run the school with an eye to every detail. Now he was expected to leave it. "To pull up stakes," he wrote the alumni, "and to move from the old study where four rectors have wrought, is not without pain."

The end came suddenly. At fifty-seven the energy never flagged, yet in retrospect one could see signs and omens. At a dinner in 1936, given by the alumni to mark the twenty-five years of his rectorship, he had spoken in highly personal terms of his own shy and unpromising youth. "My natural understanding," he said, "has always been with failure…A persistent creed that the miscreant is always entitled to tenderness, that the so-called bad boy is probably better than yonder ever-so-good man, has leaped over the years—those pompous thirties and those prim forties; and mercy possesses me." Later he wrote of the school as a place for the young—"the young chronologically and the young in heart. There will come a time for each of us when Mother Nature will assert her claim."

He spoke of "the pathos of last things," and his mind, in this season, turned back lovingly to the Coits and to the long history of the school in which they had played so commanding a part. Charles Wheeler Coit, the first rector's oldest son, was invited to spend several summer weeks at the school in the Prophet's Chamber at Hargate. A few months later Drury received from Ruth Coit, Henry Coit's niece, a letter which in a few touching words brought harmony to all of the school's history. "Being a very old lady and at the moment in bed but not ill, I believe if you were here I would put my arms around you, because I am so genuinely glad of what you are accomplishing and have accomplished for St. Paul's School."

A month later, on his regular rounds of the Infirmary, he spoke to the school doctor of a peculiar numbness in his arm. It was diagnosed as a coronary thrombosis. Silently, with his wife, Drury departed for a hospital in Boston. From his bed he carried on correspondence, dictated to his secretary notes on routine school matters, prepared a pre-Lenten message to the neighborhood congregation of the Old Chapel. But the angel of death was standing by. Six days after his arrival in Boston, in the night-hours, in the sixtieth year of his age, Samuel Drury died.

11

Nash and the War Years

1938–1946

Ⅰn the Big Study next morning Henry Kittredge announced the news to a stunned and disbelieving school.

For the funeral, the Chapel was filled by boys, masters, returning alumni, and outstanding figures of the educational world. These last had come to pay their tribute to a man who had been an exemplar in his role as schoolmaster and had so often challenged them with his fresh and powerfully-expressed ideas. The choir sang the school anthem, "O Pray for the Peace"—not that Drury had ever craved peace for himself—indeed, he had feared that in the little Jerusalem over which he presided there might be too much peace—or at least too much easy contentment. The last notes of the recessional, as they died away on the organ, were picked up by the Chapel bells, and floated over the file of silent marchers mounting the hill to the school burying ground. There Bishop Dallas of New Hampshire intoned the committal service: "From henceforth, blessed are the dead."

Immediately after, a Trustees' meeting was convoked in the Bishop's house in Concord. Henry Kittredge was appointed Acting Rector. The memorial resolution passed by the Board, bearing the mark of John Dallas's rugged Scots rhetoric, included in its praise a tribute to the fortitude with which Drury had carried on "when misunderstanding made his position as rector trying and even hard." Thus to the end Drury remained a figure seen amid controversy, his scars remembered along with his accomplishments. He would have wanted it that way.

Kittredge reads Reports in the Big Study.

At first there was little for Kittredge to do except to keep the ship steady and to carry on projects which Drury had set in train. But he was too proud a man, and too singular in his own gifts, to rest in anybody's shadow. The Acting Rector's tone began to pervade the school—cheerful, tolerant, wisely humorous. The man who had so long delighted Lower Schoolers now held his larger constituency in bemused suspense as he commented in Study Hall on matters large and small. The understated New England speech, the angular gestures, the eyebrows quick to rise in warning of some quip to follow, or—not to be missed—the rare flashes of anger: all these marked a man who did not shrink from being at center stage.

Yet something made Kittredge hold back. He did not want to be rector and he so informed the Trustees. There was, however, an old friend, a roommate of Harvard days, whom he felt qualified and ready for the post. Too observant of the niceties to press the name of a personal friend on the Trustees, Kittredge remained silent. His outspoken wife, Gertrude Kittredge, did not share these scruples. Glad to serve a good cause—and perhaps to relieve the growing pressures upon her husband—she suggested the friend's name to the Board, not (we may suppose) without a glowing account of his virtues.

So it was that the name of Norman Burdett Nash, Professor of Christian Ethics at the Episcopal Theological School in Cambridge, first enters the annals of St. Paul's.

Kittredge continued happily as Acting Rector, and at the regular Board meeting of November 1938, Nash's candidacy was discussed. At a special meeting that same month he was elected Drury's successor.

Nash had informed the Board that he was a liberal and that he had ideas of his own which he was not likely to change. Kittredge confirmed that he would bring "a new point of view, new methods of procedure, a whole set of ideas to keep us in touch with the changing complexion of the times." So Millville braced itself for the new arrival. The Rectory was soon teeming with Nash daughters and nieces, and a buzzing intellectual atmosphere took over. Meals were served at the Rectory hospitably to a broad diversity of visitors and guests, but were always hurried, as if the Rector could not spend himself on small talk, or wait to get on to the next task. Mrs. Nash began taking in boys recuperating from illnesses, making the Rectory a halfway house between their release from the Infirmary and their return to full school life. The Nashes' tastes were plain; their watchword, frugality. Returning alumni, remembering the Rectory of Drury days, found the place oddly informal.

Boys saw a preoccupied and rapidly-moving figure, one who did not suffer fools gladly and indeed sometimes seemed not to suffer them at all. Yet they respected the new Rector, and took his austerity in stride. They learned quickly to accept him as a just disciplinarian and rarely protested the expulsions he felt forced to make. "Norman the Foreman" became his sobriquet. He was also known as "Norman the Doorman" because of the proficiency with which he closed an interview when he felt the point had been made.[1]

The autumn of 1939, when Nash took over, coincided with the outbreak of war in Europe. For a year it seemed a remote disturbance, one in which the fortunes of the United States—far less of the small community of Millville—were not significantly engaged. At home the long ravages of the Depression years still showed in mass unemployment and a lethargic economy. The new Rector's first call was for stringency in school management and for simplicity in the life-style of the students.

The notable group of old masters who had come to the school in the 1890s were now at retirement age. Peck, Nelson, and White withdrew in 1940 and 1941. A firm retirement policy was now in place (along with a decent pension system), and Nash was spared the grumbling and sniping which had fallen to Drury in his early years. Even so there were difficulties when the firm hand of the Doorman became manifest. One of these men claimed himself mortally offended by the abruptness with which the Rector dissented from his views at a masters' meeting. Another let it be known he had been forced unceremoniously into retirement, though age and deafness made him an unapt teacher.

If the Old Guard was effectively defanged, some younger masters carried on the traditionalist cause. A small group of mutually supportive dissidents gained credence for their views among gifted students whose friendship they especially cultivated. Nash objected to the criticism thus engendered. The school, he said, was too small a place to harbor even a "loyal" opposition. He also felt that cliques of the brighter boys would develop a new snobbishness.

Meeting the problem head-on in frank interviews with the men concerned, Nash made his views known. When a few of these men left, it was, whatever their personal wounds, with-

---

1. President of the sixth form during Nash's first year, a student who admired and helped educate him to SPS ways, was John V. Lindsay, later to become the noted congressman and dynamic mayor of New York City.

out the agitated repercussions following similar dismissals in earlier days. That Nash should have escaped the kind of at tacks leveled against the young Drury in similar circumstances was due in part to the times. The school was now a far more stable and well-adjusted community than in the immediate post-Coit era. The lingering Depression, and then the advancing war in Europe, helped keep attention fixed on larger issues. Nevertheless there were some persistent doubts about the degree of compatibility between the old school and this driving new rector. A new member of the Board, Henry Laughlin, jovial Boston potentate, head of the mighty publishing house of Houghton Mifflin, liked to claim in later years that he had made Norman Nash Rector of St. Paul's; and that he had had to make him Bishop of Massachusetts to get him out.

Nash looked impatiently on the curriculum (as he did on almost everything else), but the time was not ripe for a thoroughgoing revision. Kittredge's prescription for many-sided teachers, rather than a multiplication of courses, still ruled. Nash's contribution was not a new course of study, but greater stress on contemporary political and economic problems. The school's aim, he said in 1940, should be to teach students that "history is now in the making, and that past and present are continuous stages in a living process, of which he himself is a part, and in which he must bear responsibility in years to come." Events were soon to prove that the young men of that day were indeed "a part of history."

The Rector was at his best in his re-examination and redefinition of the school's mission. Others were asking what purpose was served by a church school like St. Paul's. Nash did not consider the answer easy or self-evident. The public schools at that time were in a relatively good state of health. They were doing their job in their own way, and Nash stated bluntly that in the opinion of many the independent school was a vestigial survival which would not last much longer.

His own conviction, as he looked forth from Millville upon the dark ideological movements of Fascism and Nazism,

Norman B. Nash, fifth Rector. They called him "Norman the Foreman."

was that the independent school was not less, but more important, then ever. Caesar was ascendant, both in the form of demos and of dictator, making claims upon the whole man. To withstand these claims was the modern mission of St. Paul's. It could only be fulfilled by an institution truly independent and based on religious faith.

From the beginning St. Paul's had seen itself as something apart from the mainstream secular life of the country. The school's purpose at the beginning was to subject young men to a moral and rational environment, impressing upon their still-malleable natures a particular image of virtue. Partly this was to be done through the insensible pressure of natural beauty, in an ordered community of civilized persons. But always beyond that was the sense of God's immanent role in human affairs. Through the pastoral period it was enough that God, like a Greek deity, be present at the feast, an intimate part of young men's games and studies.

As the nineteenth century advanced, the question of the school's religious base was put more explicitly. Samuel Eliot, most scholarly and eloquent of Trustees, speaking at the dedication of the New Chapel in 1888, declared that "education, real education, must be religious." No matter where it begins or where it ends, he said, "there is no part of it so simple or so highly wrought that it can safely forego relations with the infinite." And again: "Literature is not wholly itself, nor science, nor art, nor any branch of human learning, unless its divine connections are followed out." There the great argument rested, until world upheavals forced a fresh interpretation.

For Nash, as the demonic forces of World War II were unleashed, the secular ideal of citizenship was no longer adequate for the maintenance of a civilized social order. Allegiance given unquestioningly to a national leader was ending in atrocities accepted without shame. "We are sure," said Nash, "that the man is more than the citizen, and indeed that only the man who knows himself as a member of the commonwealth which is eternal can offer the state a citizenship loyal, intelligent, critical." And only a core of such men—men such as a school like St. Paul's sought to nurture—could preserve the state from the ancient idolatry of itself.

The war came to the United States with the attack on Pearl Harbor in December 1941. Nothing at the school, as nothing in the world outside, would escape its tremendous changes and upheavals. At Millville the first changes were small in scale. Boys learned to do household chores and kept the grounds in place of men who were drafted. Such an ancient (and already outmoded) custom as wearing starched collars on Sunday was discarded as laundry services were reduced. With gasoline rationed, horses were recalled from honorable retirement to draw the crew barges to Long Pond, and for lack of fuel the power launches of the coaches gave way to one-man shells.

A little later the wider measures of wartime hit the school. Students were fingerprinted. Fire drills and air raid precautions were regularly carried out. Blackouts were imposed—not altogether welcomed by the boys when it was found that studies could be continued uninterruptedly in spite of them. Meanwhile on the surrounding hills groups of masters kept watch against possible enemy bombers. As in World War I, lawns were dug up for "victory gardens." Coal was accumulated in massive piles, a precaution against frigid wartime winters.

A course in aeronautics was offered. The same Gerald Chittenden who had formed drill squads in the earlier war now lectured on discipline and *esprit de corps.*

The Rector, nevertheless, cast a cold eye upon anything he considered a sign of hysteria. In chapel he conspicuously refrained from calling on the Lord for victory; it was enough to pray for steadfastness and courage. He resisted, as well, the pressure to downgrade the classics and other forms of liberal learning in favor of subjects considered more "practical."

Nor did Nash relax the school's long-standing commitment to religious education. Indeed he enlarged it, believing such studies to be a vital part of a young man's preparation for war or peace. Throughout the war he continued to teach his course in Christian Ethics, dealing in vigorous, no-nonsense style with age-old dilemmas of human conduct.

Inevitably, problems of discipline arose. The ranks of young masters were rapidly depleted; the number of applicants from which promising students could be chosen was reduced; and boys in general were uneasy and restless. An unusual number of dismissals added to the turnover of students departing for training. The Upper School, with its numerous vacancies, was now more than ever a place apart, and it became a predictable generator of trouble. Because of the diminished number of sixth formers, almost everyone had as many rooms as he desired. From here so-called clubs—the Howdy Club, the Sheik Club, the Club Flamingo—extended their baleful influence. The *Horae* remarked facetiously that the Upper was "practically a Ritz Hotel—minus some service and numerous other small improvements."

For those masters who remained at their post, duty wore a

dusty face. The Rector spent long hours at his desk carrying on a correspondence with alumni, most of whom he had not even met, now scattered on battlefronts across the globe. Older masters watched young colleagues go off to distant challenges—and, when the draft age was lowered, watched sixth formers departing too—with wistful gaze. Nash quoted his great predecessor: "Education," Drury had written during another war, "is a practical midstream mission, a call to the risky task of dealing with souls—souls in the making." Schoolmasters should be "gladly aware that a little section of the battlefront is allotted to them."

Of the old boys of the school who fought on all the fronts in all the services, often leaving behind young wives and young families, whatever may be said is too little. One hundred and five of them paid the supreme sacrifice. One must believe that some element of their life at St. Paul's was with them to the end and made them part of the school's history forever.

It is only possible to speak here of one of these young men—and to let him speak for all.

John W. Garrett 2nd had come to the school as an immature student in 1940. At the end of his fifth form year he was telling his parents, "I've really enjoyed this term, and the sorrows and disappointments of other terms have paled into insignificance in the great happiness that has been mine for the past two months....I have come to realize what a wonderful place the School is, in its location, in its boys, in its opportunities....I did not want to come here. I fought the idea to the last ditch."

A year later when he was preparing to graduate, he was writing once more to his parents: "Do you remember those letters I used to write in my fourth form year—You'll see great changes in me when I come home?" And yet, he now says, there is no change. "St. Paul's is not a school which changes its students in a month or two—St. Paul's reaches down into the hearts of its boys; it plays upon their natures, their characters, their very souls—and these cannot be altered in a short time. Probably the changes will never be noticed. They will be shown, rather, in our

*John W. Garrett 2nd,
in 1942. He was not
yet twenty when his
plane crashed.*

children and our children's children—the friendship, the breed-
ing, the open-mindedness, the sense of honesty and fair play and
the desire to do and to seek after what is right."

John Garrett graduated in June 1942. He entered directly
into military aviation. Six months later a bomber he was pi-
loting suffered mechanical failure and he brought the plane
down in a crash landing. Of the crew of seven all were saved
except him. He was not yet twenty years of age.

The war ended and the school resumed its normal course, but
with grounds and buildings showing the marks of enforced
neglect, and with accumulated wartime deficits. Changes in student life—a greater informality in dress and less dependence on
services once taken for granted—were not to be reversed. The
young masters returned. The Rectory, from which the Nash
daughters and nieces had gone to war jobs and service in the
WACS, became again a center of family life.

The last year of the war had seen the students at odds with themselves and with the school. Disciplinary problems increased; scholarly standards declined. Nash pondered "the mysterious process of maturation" and hoped to ease the unrest by what he called "the benevolent pressures of school life." "We do not propose to be less patient," he told the Trustees," but we hope that we can improve our guidance and correction." Although the number of student applications had fallen to a disconcertingly low level, Nash was disposed to drop students who showed no improvement in their marks. Boys, even the sons of alumni, were not to be allowed "to flounder through a year or two of discouragement and frustration."

In the midst of dealing with these problems, in January 1946, Nash was elected Bishop of Massachusetts. No inner struggle seems to have accompanied his decision to accept, as none had accompanied his decision to come to St. Paul's in the first place. His work at the school could be considered complete. He had guided it through difficult years. War had forestalled most new initiatives; but his lively intelligence had helped keep the ship on course, and had enabled him to distinguish, almost infallibly, between the things that were transitory or fashionable and those that were likely to endure.

In their farewell the Trustees spoke of "the path through the school made by his vigorous and active step." St. Paul's could well take pride in having proven itself a large enough place to engage for seven years the energies of this good and courageous man.

As bishop, Nash lived up to his reputation for boldness. His first sermon was an advocacy of birth control as a means of family planning. In the 1950s he took his stand against the malicious innuendoes of Senator Joseph McCarthy, strongly defending young clergymen of his diocese against charges of communism.

Bishop Nash practiced, as at St. Paul's he had preached, a citizenship "loyal, intelligent, critical."

12

A Layman Rules in Zion

1947–1954

With Nash's departure the school faced once more what Henry Kittredge had called "a broken year," and once more he was called to the post of acting rector. It was a role with which he was becoming all too familiar. Not only had he filled the void after Drury's death, but in 1943, when as a result of a fall Nash was unable to function for almost a full school year, he had taken over the burden from his friend. He was now fifty-seven years old. He had known the school intimately, in all its aspects, as had only a few men in its history. He was not—despite a certain diffidence of manner and an almost excessive enjoyment of his vacations on Cape Cod—an unambitious man; nor did Gertrude Livingston, his wife, lack the intelligence or charm to shine in the largest company. This, if ever, was Henry Kittredge's hour.

The Trustees hesitated, even as they felt the need for haste. The school in that uneasy postwar world, and after the earlier hiatus in leadership, could not afford to drift. Kittredge was the obvious choice for rector but he was a layman, and the tradition of a clergyman in the post was strong. One unsuccessful effort to enlist a clergyman brought the Board back to their own vice rector. At a special meeting at the Yale Club in New York on May 22, 1947, they elected him the sixth rector of St. Paul's. This time there was no hesitancy in Kittredge's acceptance.

Did the Board consider him an interim rector, as Henry

Henry Kittredge, Rector, steps forth on a brisk morning.

Ferguson had been—a layman holding office for a brief seven years before retirement, keeping things together until the rule of a churchman could be restored? Undoubtedly some of the Trustees saw the choice in this light. But the school's larger constituency accepted Kittredge in his own right, looked joyfully on his election, and sat back to watch the show.

Kittredge's ideal image of the school was a place where, harassed by a minimum of punishments and penalties, boys would work hard and pursue a maximum variety of leisure activities. He cared for eccentricity, and he elevated tolerance to a major virtue. It was the school's aim, as he once expressed it, to attain "a genuine, natural, genial atmosphere"—a condition to which most boys would respond and some would greet as a novelty "because they had never seen anything like it before."

To a large extent he succeeded in creating such an atmosphere. He would be criticized by certain of the masters for not providing leadership or definite goals. But he was convinced that leadership was a by-product of a community functioning harmoniously, and was not imposed from above. As for goals, he assumed them to be so simple as to be self-evident. If they became complicated, they would only be illusory. Emphasis on method as opposed to substance, on procedure as opposed to underlying values, always distressed him. More accurately, it tested his forbearance and provoked his ironical humor.

Kittredge's long career as a successful teacher gave him particular ideas about the academic side of the school. "We have little faith in pains or penalties," he declared in his first Annual Report as Rector, "or in mechanical devices however ingenious." His aim was simple: to introduce more "liveliness" into recitations. He envisaged a school where boys would step across the threshold of a classroom—as not long since they had stepped across his—feeling an anticipatory thrill, and where each boy would leave the room "wiser and better than when he entered it."

For a teacher to achieve such results, scholarly degrees and formal training were not essential, he believed. What the teacher needed was "imagination, vigor, and faith in the importance of his doctrine." Methods he would invent for himself as he went along; the best technique was that which suited a man's own genius. "If he knows his subject thoroughly, he will at least stand a chance of igniting a spark now and then in a youthful brain."

One such ideal teacher Kittredge described. "He has no notion of discipline but goes through the day as though no boy would ever misbehave." He had the reputation of being very lenient. "He marks the boys easier than other teachers do; but I notice," said Kittredge, "that they do just as well on college examinations as those who have been prepared by the rest of us." Some of them even caught the idea of behaving without being made to do so!

As he professed an almost subversive disdain for formal methods of teaching, so he treated lightly the principles of administration. Here he is discussing the delegation of authority: One of his aims, he had said, was to reduce as quickly as possible some of the stress and strain of school life on masters and boys. "This was one of the broad and vague expressions into which one is sometimes betrayed in an expansive moment after a good dinner, and in truth I had at the moment no plan in mind for achieving this happy end. But none was necessary. The vice rector was there and obviously thought well of the idea, and in a week or two presented a plan for bringing it to pass."

The school buildings were in deplorable condition after years of wartime neglect. An eye to economy, as well as a deep-rooted reluctance to make personal demands, left the Rectory in a state more satisfying to Kittredge's New England conscience than his wife's tastes. More than the usual cases of leaky roofs, broken sewer lines and heating failures worried him very little. He dealt with such problems, one at a time, as if they were part of a different world from that he normally inhabited. Yet even in dealing with these he found the occasion for outbursts of his characteristic style. A crack had appeared in the Powerhouse chimney. "It took nearly ten thousand dollars," said he cheerfully to his Board, "to plug that disastrous fissure."

Yet in at least one instance he was pleased by new evidence of efficiency in the school office. A few years previously there had arrived a young man with a genius for getting hitherto uncollected facts into intelligible order. He was "very scientific and up to date," the Rector reported to his Trustees. Kittredge knew a good thing when he saw it. The name of the young man was William A. Oates. We shall hear of him again in this narrative.

In regard to the boys, Kittredge took what must seem an almost perverse delight in praising the student who was less than brilliant in his studies or conformist in his habits. He liked "the

Dispensing "excuses" on a Cricket Holiday.

plodders, a dozen or so in every form, to whom geometry is a riddle and the understanding of a poem a battle against odds....They are modest and cheerful, they are sympathetic supervisors in the houses occupied by younger boys; they are generous and sometimes distinguished athletes, and in every phase of the life of the school they pull their full weight. They leave the school a better place for their having been members of it."

"We must be," Kittredge continued, "what Henry Adams called 'patient students of human error,' and if we persevere, by the time these willing workers have been in the school for two or three years, they will have learned the age-old problem of how to study well...and will pocket their diplomas with the rest."

From his wry appreciation of the odd boy and the misfit, Kittredge derived his hatred of intolerance in all forms. During the war instances of hazing had occurred, and there was always below the surface of boarding school life the danger of brutal or unfeeling conduct. Even where physical harassment was not involved, hazing could be subtly cruel. One master was known as "Creeping Jesus," another as "Prosperity" because he was always just around the corner. The seemingly innocuous sobriquet of "Deen" was applied to one boy because his complexion seemed to resemble wartime's Aberdeen proving ground.

Against this trend in school life Henry Kittredge blazed away in school assemblies, and in an early Annual Report spoke out eloquently. "Youth is a cruel time," he said, "cruel and conservative." Happily the days were past when being a new boy in itself justified abuse. "But a vigorous ghost of the old savagery remains in the maltreatment to which queerness is sometimes subjected. To change this intolerance to tolerance is the schoolmaster's hardest duty—hardest and most important. Until it has been learned, a boy's Christianity is a hollow shell and the process of civilizing him has not begun."

When punishment was required, Kittredge could be lenient—some thought too lenient. "We may indeed consider ourselves children of a world in which a degree of frailty may still be found," he told the alumni. But the fact that he took so much of life on faith led him into swift and summary—occasionally too swift and summary—action when he felt his faith betrayed or the margin of his tolerance exceeded. Dismissals, coming from one normally so genial, could cause a stir within the faculty. But there was no apparent remorse on his side, and his summations could be as succinct as they were final. One year's sixth form had achieved the highest marks in the school's history; but "their behavior," Kittredge reported, "was not on a par with their industry."

The school did indeed seem to be a happy community. It was as if something of the earlier years had returned, years when the first Coit was young and created an Arcadian setting. Student life was woven of many-colored strands, as new institutions took form or old ones were revived. The *Pelican*, a weekly

*"Patsy" Kittredge
at the Sixth Form
Dance. She "tripped
the light fantastic."*

newspaper established in 1945, was now challenging the cen-
tury-old preeminence of the *Horae Scholasticae*.[1] But like other
aspects of the school in those innocent years, it was good-humored in tone, not the shrill or mordantly witty publication it
came to be during the 1960s.

Its editors were finding plenty to report in such goings-on as
the school dances. The midwinter dance weekend of 1954 saw,
for example, the most numerous female guests, and probably the
most sprightly, ever gathered at the school. Seventy girls, arriving in Concord, were brought to Millville in hay-wagons, and
deposited before a blazing fire in the little house that had been
built as a memorial to Willard Scudder. Warmed, and with pre-
liminary greetings and assignments completed, the girls and their
escorts were served a light collation. There followed an informal
dance, a sort of early discotheque, with music supplied (accord-

---

1. First editor of the Pelican was James W. Kinnear III, future Board president. Its declared purpose was to reproduce "the activities, opinions, and prejudices" of the boys of
St. Paul's School.

ing to the *Pelican*) by "Peter Rabbit's handmade victrola."

The next day, a Saturday, there was a hockey game as there had always been, and the traditional Missionary Society fair. It was "the gayest and most successful ever." In the oak-ceilinged dining room of the Upper School, with the founder and past rectors looking down from the wall, the weekend's principal entertainment unfolded. "As regards decoration," the Pelican observed, "simplicity was the keynote." But small tables, intimately lighted by candles, were placed at the edges of the dance-floor; and as the evening wore on, Mrs. Kittredge was very much in evidence. A delighted and delightful presence, she knew the name of every girl (she had arranged for all seventy of them to stay at masters' houses), and was not herself averse, in her husband's phrase, to "tripping the light fantastic."

Sunday brought its quieter amusements; until the evening came on and after the brief, moving service in the dim Chapel, all the girls were hustled off.

About this time the Thanksgiving Crawl was invented. A young instructor in Spanish and history, Señor José Antonio G. Ordoñez y Montalvo, made his first run to Long Pond soon after arriving at the school. "I have loved ever since," he said, "the trails, the water, the hills, the little valleys." And so on one Thanksgiving Day after chapel, under Señor Ordoñez's direction, the crawl began. (It was a kind of trot, the forerunner of modern cross-country running at St. Paul's, and perhaps an anticipation of the "jogging" which a dozen years later was to sweep the country.) Before starting out, the participants joined in a little ceremony on the Chapel lawn. The first stanza of "O God Our Help in Ages Past" was sung. This was done in order that all who took part would have the courage to finish.

The intrepid group, leaving the Chapel, rounded the Lower School Pond, crossed some fields, and entered a dark wood. Coming out at the foot of Jerry Hill, they proceeded to Long Pond. Here the last stanza of "O God Our Help" was sung, for moral encouragement, before the homeward trek by another

"The saddest change…" Canoeing on the Lower School Pond had disappeared before the 1950s.

route. The whole passage was made—and would be for years to come—at a slow pace, permitting ample opportunity to savor the changing views and the beauties of the November woods.

Kittredge found pleasure in the weeks long considered anathema at the school—the slush season of March. Then, as he said, sports are largely unscheduled and the athletic program is casual and miscellaneous. It was a time when boys could develop their own talents and follow their own fancy. That canoeing was no more in fashion was "the saddest change that has taken place in the school." But he was able to encourage one of the old leisure-time pursuits, the building of huts in the school's outer domain.

A youth of ironical vein, graduating during these years, caught accurately in a memoir for the *New Yorker* the spirit that Kittredge sought to cultivate. He recalled the feeling of ease and casual abundance at the school— "showers that ran in a never-ending stream of hot water, food of such extraordinary delicacy that it could frequently be eaten without ketchup." There were teachers, even, who seemed to have taken up their task "with at least a semblance of vocation"; there were "lots of trees, and grass, and woods, and ponds. We used to skip football practice some afternoons to go roaming through the woods in the back of the playing fields, looking for a supposed secret way to a nearby village." The village was never found, "but it was nice to go crashing through the woods, even in November…even when the sun went down very early and the trees were bare and the ground was hard, and everything in the world seemed brittle— except us, I think."

More serious events during the Kittredge years were not lacking, but for the most part seemed to happen without stir, as if generated by the same Fortune that regulated the seasons or the unpredictable dispositions of boys. "We don't have to invent changes," said the Rector in an address to the alumni. "They are pushed on us by circumstances. All we have to do is keep limber and manipulate the inevitable."

The War, the G.I. Bill of Rights, shortages of men and material, and then the postwar boom all had their effects on St. Paul's. They left their impress on the curriculum—a new emphasis on art and music instruction, a course in public affairs and American democracy; also an increase in scholarships, abandonment of the old waiting list for admissions, and preparation for a college scene grown so competitive as to cast its shadow backward over the last two years of study at the school. Meanwhile other changes occurred in the buildings and the physical environment.

The first postwar construction project was a memorial which Trustees and alumni, after prolonged discussion, decided should take the form of an auditorium. The old gathering place atop the gymnasium, built in 1878, had long since lost its usefulness. The architectural firm of Ralph Adams Cram was engaged, but the heavily adorned Gothic style of their design, and its suggested location on the site of two old clapboard cottages, caused the plans to be rejected and the contract canceled. Next the architect Richard A. Kimball was asked to try his hand.

He won approval with his design for a building in the Georgian style, placed behind the Schoolhouse, later to be flanked by classrooms so as to form an academic quadrangle. Difficulties in raising funds for the project, combined with lingering shortages and rising prices, put off the completion until June 1951. Alumni entering for the dedication ceremonies found themselves in a beautifully detailed antechamber, with the names of the war dead engraved upon a single large slate panel

The Old Chapel in the 1950s. The Trustees voted to tear it down.

and a moving inscription running as a frieze above. The auditorium sloped comfortably, large enough to hold the entire school. Gone were the creaking floors and the squeaky chairs that for so many decades had drowned out concerts and made the words of lecturers inaudible.

A further initiative almost resulted in disaster. At their meeting of January 1952, the Trustees voted to demolish the Old Chapel. It was their gesture toward reducing maintenance costs. First building erected at the school, gift of the founder and embodiment of treasured memorials, here the first rector had guided and blessed generations of St. Paul's boys. It was still being used for smaller school services and as a place of worship for the surrounding neighborhood. A protest from masters and alumni caused the decision to be reversed at the next meeting of the Board. That it should have been taken in the first place suggests how far the school's history, and perhaps how far its religious values, had declined.

The country was at that time passing through the ordeal of the Korean war. This was not yet Vietnam, but it was a portent of things to come. Kittredge summed up the reactions of the students: "They see themselves in combat and it depresses them." How different from the zeal with which the young had faced the wars of 1914 and 1941!

In the school's backyard another conflict was played out, placing its vital interests in opposition to the citizens of Concord. A muted antagonism of some Concordians had long been sensed, and now it focused on the school's rowing at Long Pond, source of the city's drinking water. Kittredge and his wife had been doing much to bring the capital city into closer contact with St. Paul's, but such efforts did not preclude the town's closing the pond to the school's use. The board of trade and the majority of local doctors found no danger of pollution and called for the pond's being reopened to St. Paul's rowers.

At a climactic hearing in March 1952—the largest in Concord's history—Kittredge made an eloquent appeal stressing the school's long involvement in the Concord community; the economic benefits of school-provided jobs, purchases, and bank deposits; the courtesies extended to the citizens through use of the school ponds and tennis courts in summer; and the school camp harboring annually some fifty Concord boys. All was in vain. Passions were beyond the reach of reason. "A small minority," shouted one member of the opposition, "wants to play in our drinking water." Three weeks later the vote of the city council went 16 to 4 against boating on Long Pond. The school faced the end of one of its most salutary and long-lived sporting activities.

Under Drury's far-seeing eye, however, steps had been taken against just such a crisis. At his urging almost all the land surrounding the two Turkey ponds had been purchased by the school. He had envisaged a future rowing course in this area, within a ten-minute walk of the school. Now was the time to put his dream to the test.

The frost was barely out of the ground when a road to Big Turkey was cleared. A number of large pines along the way were cut down to make a dock; a pile of sawdust, left over from the logging operations after the hurricane of 1938, was leveled to form a place for spectators. Barges and shells were brought down from Long Pond—some of them carried on foot by rowing enthusiasts—and racks were made for them under the trees. By Race Day a course had been opened, considerably shorter than the old one, shallow, and with its waters strewn with debris. But it was a beginning, and it kept the tradition of rowing alive. Massive public works necessary to make the course into one truly adequate would have to wait for another day.

In this period came large—and mostly unanticipated—additions to the school's endowments. No one could have been more surprised than Henry Kittredge when he turned out to be the beneficiary of more sizable gifts than any rector before him. In rapid succession a bequest of $1.5 million came from Edward S. Harkness; more than half a million was added by the bequest

Henry and Gertrude Kittredge in the Rectory, shortly before his retirement.

of Hamilton Fish Webster, a graduate of the golden 1870s. Most extraordinary, a fabulously wealthy lady who had never visited the school, Sylvia Wilks, divided her estate among various institutions, leaving the little colony at Millville $2 million the richer.

Over these accessions Henry Kittredge presided, bemused and impressed. An alumnus congratulated him on a particularly successful year. "But will there ever again be such an avalanche of coin?" asked the Rector.

The Trustees, determined not to be caught again with a choice made under pressure, had taken steps to assure a smooth succession. Kittredge had been rector only three years when they began their search. In ways which will presently be related, they settled upon Matthew Madison Warren, rector of

All Saints Episcopal Church in Atlanta, Georgia, providing for him a year of study abroad in preparation for his new work, and a year at the school as vice rector and rector-elect. The time for his taking up residence at the school was now at hand, and neither of the men involved found it an easy situation. But they managed to remain on good terms for the most part, these two strong figures dwelling in a small world, the one waiting to take over the reins, the other completing his long service.

At a crowded dinner at the Plaza Hotel in New York alumni and their wives gathered to say farewell and to express their affection for the Kittredges. Displaying the gifts that had made her so long a luminous presence at the tea table and a star upon the stage of the Master Players, "Patsy" Kittredge charmed the audience. Henry told stories about boys he remembered, and the evening was a great success.

As the last spring unfolded, there was no strain in the farewells at the school. Kittredge would have been made uneasy by emotional displays. Besides, he was delighted to be returning to his beloved Barnstable on Cape Cod. After forty years of responsibility at a boys' boarding school, the prospect of idleness was, he said, "sheer heaven."

The parting gift of the Trustees was a pair of marine binoculars, through which the ex-rector could observe the Cape Cod birds or watch for wrecks offshore. Upon this son of Harvard, Yale conferred an honorary degree. "Humane in instinct," read the citation, "gifted with humor, wise in administration." The *New York Herald Tribune* noted the retirement of a great teacher. "He threw out in abundance," it said, those "generous hints" which could be considered the substance of all true education. "His subject was English, but it might have been almost anything, for the example of the man, the wisdom implicit in his bearing and action, was the contribution which inspired above everything else his students' minds."

At Barnstable the little house on Pine Lane to which he had gone so often for refreshment and rest during his years of work became now the center of his life during the four seasons. Set a little apart from the house was his study, with its large desk, its books, its walls covered with prints of sailing vessels. Here, in letters written in his elegant small handwriting, he kept touch with his many friends, and with the fruits of his wide reading filled the pages of his leather-bound "common-place books." In the barn back of the house he would go over lovingly, like a man sorting out his treasure, pieces of driftwood collected on the beaches. He returned rarely to the school, and when he died in 1967 it was as one who had enjoyed life fully and was ready to depart.

PART THREE

13

Decade of Reform

1954–1964

❧

The little group of Trustees setting out in 1951 to find the successor to Henry Kittredge delegated one of their number to visit Atlanta. There, they had heard, was a rising figure of the Episcopal Church. John R. McLane, a Board member of almost thirty years standing, found himself in All Saints. It was a large church, its congregation including many of the city's wealthiest citizens; about six hundred members had just turned out to hear its rector preach. Afterwards, McLane introduced himself as an emissary from St. Paul's, immediately broaching the idea of Warren's becoming headmaster. Matthew Warren allowed that he knew of St. Paul's. One summer he had motored over from his cottage on the New Hampshire shore to visit the chapel. As for his leaving All Saints, he was strongly disinclined.

McLane was not the last Trustee to make the journey south. Several months later Laughlin and Dickey, the Board's most influential members, invited the rector of All Saints to dine with them at a leading Atlanta hotel. Warren accepted, but insisted that he be the host and that dinner be held at the Driving and Riding Club, inner sanctum of Atlanta's elite, to which rectors of All Saints were members, apparently, by divine right. "Gentlemen," said Warren, as they settled into these comfortable surroundings, "I am a drinking man. If you have no further interest in me, that is all right. But I am now going to order a martini." Laughlin and Dickey confessed that in the expectation of a dry evening they had fortified themselves appropriately before coming to the club. In the circumstances, however, they were not averse to accepting another drink.

The talk at dinner was along general lines, but retiring afterwards to the rectory of All Saints, they got down to business. Dickey opened the conversation abruptly. "Do you like boys?" he asked. "Name me one," said Matthew Warren, "and I'll tell you whether I like him or not." The three men talked until past midnight. It was evident the discussion had not been concluded. Rather against his will, Warren was persuaded to make a visit to the school. He was shocked by what struck him as its "overgrown and run-down" appearance. "Don't take it," his wife Rebecca said; "it will be too much."

At a special meeting of the Board on December 16, 1951, Matthew Warren was elected rector. Overcoming his doubts and reconciled to the break with his Atlanta parish, he accepted. During the third longest of the school's rectorships, and in times of extraordinary turbulence, he would never find the school "too much" for his faith and his reforming zeal.

Warren's first proposal—and his first bout with the Trustees—was on the subject of tuition. After having stood at $1,400 for twenty-two years, it had remained since 1947 at $1,600. With the exception of Memorial Hall no general drive for funds had been conducted among the alumni since the 1920s. This overcautious approach to school finances resulted in an outward aspect of things at odds with the institution's reputation and its underlying wealth.

Nash, characteristically, had wanted to lower the tuition, and many of the Trustees took pride in the school's lack of ostentation. They remembered from their own school days such austerities as fitful heating and outmoded plumbing. The idea of bringing everything up to scratch seemed expensive—and not quite in the St. Paul's tradition. But Warren, speaking for a different constituency, knew that prospects visiting the school would not be impressed by traditions of that sort.

He began his renovations with the Rectory. "I hope it has not been a shock to you," Warren wrote the president of his Board

A Driving Force—Matthew M. Warren with Rebecca Warren in the Rectory garden.

after he had first seen the results. "We found it impossible to stop anywhere." Not only had thorough repairs been made to the structure, but a new style of decorating prevailed. Worn oriental rugs gave way to wall-to-wall carpeting; new upholstery took the place of somber and slightly-frayed velours. With the same zeal for what was modern and up-to-date, the Rector was prepared to renovate other public areas of the school.

President of the Board was now Henry Laughlin, the witty Bostonian already referred to. He had a deep love for St. Paul's, coupled with a determination that it should not change too rapidly or too conspicuously. "You drive a very spirited horse and it will be hard for the poor old Trustees to keep you in sight," Laughlin wrote the Rector; "I do not believe the world can, or should be, made over in less than the statutory seven days." There was a slight note of warning in the words, and now on the question of a tuition raise he and other members of the Board stood firm. A low tuition (but not too low, as Nash discovered) had long represented something old and fundamental in the St. Paul's ethos—the idea that the school was not just for the rich—and that even the rich should not flaunt their wealth.

Warren countered with the argument that St. Paul's should charge at least as much as comparable schools and that it should show to the world a face befitting its constituency. The less advantaged, in his view, would have access through scholarships provided from an ample endowment. The school he envisaged was one where the rich would be pressed to give, and from which the poor would not be excluded. Besides, he wanted higher tuition to enable him to raise faculty salaries to what he considered a competitive and also a dignified level.

The issue was joined, and at the Board meeting of January 1955 the Rector won his point—as important for what it signified of his attitude and approach to education as it was in its effect on the immediate budget. Despite Laughlin's opposition, the fee was raised to $1,800. Subsequently Laughlin instructed the school's business manager to hold up the public announcement. Warren was furious. A heated telephone conversation took place, and the next morning Laughlin, having come up from Boston, was at the door of the Rector's study.

The confrontation cleared the air. Afterwards there was full, if sometimes stormy, cooperation between the two men. Warren, from that day, was plainly marked to be a strong rector.

He turned next to the school's physical environment. The old Middle was already in process of demolition, and he led in replacing it with ample new quarters for students and masters. A firm of outside experts named at his request marked both the Big Study and the old Lower for demolition. He then

The Rector with president of the Board Henry Laughlin and Benjamin Neilson, president of the sixth form and future Trustee, at Anniversary of the Centennial year.

turned to a major—and for the school quite radical—construction project. This was the building of a modern gymnasium with an indoor "cage" for sports.

How could such a thing be necessary? For generations St. Paul's students had lived with the myth that in an abundance of outdoor space and a vigorous and bracing climate, God had provided everything essential for the physical well-being of the young. Skepticism was heightened when it was discovered that central to the new exercise house would be facilities for basketball. "Not basketball!" cried a sizable minority of the Trustees. No less disturbing was the fact that locker rooms and showers for the whole student body were to be included. The latter was in direct contravention to the long-standing custom of having boys keep their "old clothes" in their rooms, to which they imparted a characteristic and nostalgically remembered odor.

The school's hundredth anniversary was approaching, and Warren suggested that the principal fund-raising activity be devoted to paying for the new exercise house. Alumni questioned whether this was a project sufficiently grand for the occasion. Laughlin was "flabbergasted" by the sum of money—$3.2 million—which would be required. The alumni agreed to raise the money, nevertheless, leaving it to the Board to choose the purpose for which it would be used. The Board, in settling for the gymnasium and cage, gave Warren another victory.

The large new building was erected on the main route between the center of the school and the Lower Grounds, an unadorned barnlike structure of cement block, to which was attached a sort of oversized Quonset hut enclosing a fine space for track and tennis. In the main building, beside the basketball courts, were facilities for boxing, wrestling, shooting, and other diversions. A handsome central space (the Gates Room) was well adapted to entertaining visiting teams and a variety of other school functions. The building, as much as anything else, symbolized the seventh rector's concern for contemporary social mores and his sympathy with the youth of his day.

Other building enterprises followed. Structures that had withstood staunchly the hard usage of years were refurbished room by room. Hargate was made over into an arts center, and two new dining halls were attached to the rear of the Upper, thus centralizing all kitchen facilities. Three new dormitories for twenty students each, with a house for a married master and rooms for a single, were next proposed. The architect and planner Edward L. Barnes persuaded the Board to abandon their first choice of putting them in an apple orchard outside the center of the school. Instead, he fortified the main street with a row of low buildings running on either side of the Rectory. In due course the old Lower was torn down and a new dormitory (now "Kittredge") was built along the pond.

A notable change in the landscape was achieved to complete the rowing course begun at Big Turkey Pond a few years earlier. A new, limited highway—now Interstate 89— being projected, the school convinced the authorities to skirt the school and build

Aerial photo of the completed rowing course, looking toward Little Turkey Pond, Route I-89 at center.

a bridge at the narrow neck connecting Big and Little Turkey Ponds. In exchange for a donation of land, the bridge was designed with arches wide enough to let crews pass underneath. The school then dredged what had been a marshy stream connecting the two ponds. Thus in 1958 the Turkeys were united in one sweep of unbroken water, offering an ideal rowing course within easy walking distance of the school.

On other fronts, too, the Rector was not idle.

In December 1956 he sent a memorandum to the Board informing them that the Reverend John Walker, of Detroit, would become a history teacher at the school the following autumn. Five candidates had been interviewed, and he was plainly the best. "The unusual aspect of the situation," the memorandum continued, "is that Mr. Walker is a Negro."

Thus at a stroke the Rector ended a situation that had long existed at St. Paul's. The school's admission policy had not ex-

Spectators gathered at the finish line.

cluded blacks; but the fact that no young African-Americans would apply had been accepted as a fact of life. To search out a few and to make them bear the burden of being the first seemed to Warren a dubious procedure. A black master, on the other hand, would be mature, and would prepare the way at the school for others of his race.

John Walker, whom Warren had chosen for this role, was an appealing young man, then in his early thirties, articulate, gentle in his ways, and with a clear sense of where he and his fellow blacks were going. The students found in him a first-rate teacher and a sympathetic counselor. From the alumni came a few—surprisingly few—outcries of dismay. More general, perhaps, was the tendency to treat Warren as a "controversial figure." Walker left in 1966 to become canon of the National Cathedral in Washington, and then Bishop of Washington. In 1972 he became a member of the Board of Trustees.

Two years after his coming to the school as master, the first black student, Luther Hilton Foster, took his place in the St. Paul's community.

Early in Warren's term the school was confronted by a new situation in regard to admissions. A dearth of applicants, sometimes bringing the school close to accepting all who applied, had troubled Nash and Kittredge. Now children born immediately after World War II were knocking in unprecedented numbers at the door of schools and colleges. Warren's problem became that of choice and selection.

The situation created strains with alumni, who found their sons frequently rejected. Henry Laughlin took up the cause, urging the Rector to be more considerate of the alumni. Warren only promised that in the immediate future there would be "no less torture" for them and for him.

As a non-alumnus, a relative stranger to Millville, Warren was in a difficult position. He was deeply imbued with a sense of

John Walker—Master, Trustee, Bishop; always a wise counselor.

the school as an organic structure, embodying the past as well as the future. He was not intent (despite frequent charges to the contrary) on making St. Paul's a mere powerhouse of the intellectual elite. To admit boys clearly capable of academic work of a high order was, of course, desirable. But if St. Paul's needed scholars, it also needed artists, debaters, good writers, athletes. Excellence, to be a meaningful concept, must embrace excellence over a wide diversity of fields, not in studies alone.

Warren denied that scholarships were being used to entice only bright students. They were being used to make possible the enlistment of as many students as possible—alumni and non-alumni, the academically brilliant and the less brilliant— among those selected by the admissions committee. Moreover, Warren remained a strong supporter of maintaining the two lower forms of the school. The ultimate development of these younger boys was difficult to predict, and St. Paul's was thought for this reason to be at a competitive disadvantage with other, four-year schools.

In another way the flood of available students was causing strains. As colleges found their number of applicants soaring, they rejected many workaday students, however attractive in themselves or valuable to the community. Among these, inevitably, were graduates of St. Paul's and other similar schools. The same alumni who were insisting that their young be admitted to the school, were now berating the school because they were rejected by the college of their choice.

Warren's restless drive for reform led him to reexamine all the educational and social processes of the school. In long sessions with his advisors he raked over the pattern of existing courses. Broadened fields of knowledge and an explosion of new techniques were evident. The "holy five" of the old curriculum—mathematics, English, science, language, and history—were not capable of containing the new flood of knowledge and would within a few years break down into a list of almost a hundred courses. Accompanying this growth was the need to reorganize school life so as to make for more unbroken time, more opportunity for individual study, more leisure for a boy "to explore the notion of himself."

An "independent studies" program was initiated, permitting students in their sixth form year to free themselves from normal academic routines and, under the supervision of a master, to work on projects of their choosing—at the school or away. In another initiative, the Advanced Studies Program put the school facilities, including its ablest teachers, at the disposal of New Hampshire high school youths during a summer session. The effects of this on the regular curriculum were subtle but lasting. Emphasis on getting to the core of a matter in long, packed sessions brought in new concepts of teaching, which soon were being felt in regular term-time classes. Moreover the presence of girls in these sessions brought a novel touch. Their presence, wrote Matthew Warren, "added greatly to the interest of everyone, particularly the boys."

In the athletic program Warren responded to the same pressures for wider options and for new forms of activity. So hallowed a sport as football was beginning to lose its appeal. Soccer, and then lacrosse, were becoming increasingly popular. More profoundly, the club system of intramural sports, cherished in Millville for three-quarters of a century, showed signs of obsolescence.

It was easy at first to blame the Rector for these changing preferences. But when a committee of the Trustees was appointed to look broadly into the athletic program, they observed for themselves what had already been reported by the administration. Sport was still compulsory for all, but a greater variety of activities was being pursued and a large number of games were being played against outside schools. At a Board meeting of April 1958 the value of the club system was seriously discussed. Two years later the Trustees proposed varsity teams for each sport, with the club system being operative only for the lower teams. The report was tabled, but forces of change could not be stopped.

The emphasis on outside games was not a return to the ath-

letic craze that had troubled observers at the start of the century.
The students were less interested in creating a star system than in
breaking down the isolation in which St. Paul's had long existed.
The spirit of competitiveness was actually played down. A pro-
fusion of "minor sports" evidenced the students' individuality,
and the sports program became complex and fragmented, as the
academic program had become already.

Warren was a man of action, but he was above all a moralist, an educator, a social philosopher. He took on the role
of rector to fill it in all its dimensions, the manager of a considerable domain, but more than that, a lord spiritual of the realm,
ready to face up to the most threatening of secular powers.

Well before the outbreaks of the sixties, he knew that the
school was part of an America undergoing vast social strains.
The drive for civil rights had already begun in the South.
Other evolutions were in the making: the growing disillusionment among youth with an inherited order that did not seem
to meet its varied and often inexpressible needs; the movement
for women's rights; the urge for personal fulfillment through
art; and the growing awareness of the role of sexuality in the
development of the young human being.

"Our task," Warren said at the beginning of his rule, "re-
lates to a nation's necessity and a culture's hunger." In meeting
the challenge, the religious dimension was, he believed, paramount. It was through religion that the gifts and graces of
youth, the animal spirits of healthy human beings, could be
brought to serve ideal ends. It was in chapel that the polarities
of old and new, of tradition and change, could be reconciled.
Yet he recognized that adolescence was not a particularly religious time. "Young men in their teens feel confident. They are
vigorous, their lease on life seems to be permanent....How
hard it is to call on a Saviour when you don't feel you need one."

This sympathy with the dilemma of youth did not leave him
even in the hardest times. As students turned increasingly against

the Christian experience and view of life, he refused to believe they were being wholly negative. "I personally do not feel our students are trying to get out of something," he said when the agitations turned against chapel attendance. "The truth is, they are trying to get more significantly into something."

The Hundredth Anniversary was not only the occasion of a drive for funds. It was the occasion, also, for a reexamination of the place of the church school in contemporary society. The anniversary would not be celebrated by a succession of showy events, but by an enlargement and deepening of the

The New Chapel during the Centennial celebration.

school's traditional ceremonies. Eton's headmaster, Robert Birley, took up residence in the autumn and led a continuing seminar on the values implicit in modern secondary education. In the spring, the long-established rituals of reunion and graduation were played out on a grand scale, attracting an unprecedented influx of alumni and their families.

But it was the following autumn that the most far-reaching event took place. This was Matthew Warren's own, and he planned it with the ardor of a churchman and scholar. A symposium on the future of the church school brought representatives from two dozen schools to hear the world-famous theologian, Paul J. Tillich, present an original and striking paper on the relations between religion and education. What Tillich said that day would be read and debated over the country and in educational institutions throughout the western world. Decades later, after educational dogmas had been shattered by upheavals of the sixties, educators and churchmen would still be contemplating Tillich's paradoxes.[1]

The night of January 21, 1961, was one of the coldest in New Hampshire's twentieth century history, twenty-five degrees below zero. That evening the school was gathered in Memorial Hall, absorbed in a film, *Shake Hands with the Devil*. In the Big Study a lone master, the art teacher Bill Abbe, was in his apartment. He noticed smoke rising through the hall outside. He knocked at the doors of the few apartments carved from the labyrinth of old classrooms; finding no one there, nor anywhere else in the building, he called the fire department, gathered a few of his belongings, and made for the outdoors.

Across the street, at the Rectory, Matthew Warren was still unaware of the fire making its way through the walls of the Big Study. On the threshold, alarmed and shaken, Abbe

---

1. Even a brief discussion of Tillich's complex and subtle theme is not possible here. For a summary, see Heckscher, *St. Paul's: The Life of a New England School*, pp. 309-310.

Encased in ice, the fire-swept ruins of the Big Study.

stammered out the news. Seizing him by the shoulders, Warren demanded assurance that no one was trapped in the gathering smoke and flame.

It was already too late to save the building. Firemen battled against the insuperable odds of sub-zero temperatures, the water from their hoses freezing into grotesquely-formed icicles, while the interior became an inferno. Late in the night, flames creeping unseen through a vault of the adjacent cloister were discovered by one of the boys, who, by giving the alarm, undoubtedly saved the chapel. Awed by the fury of the conflagration, students, faculty, and all the school community stood silently in the arctic cold.

The next morning, encased in ice, the ruins of the old building stood forlornly at the center of the school. The Big Study had outlived its usefulness—classrooms, the rector's study, many of its former services, had been transferred to other buildings. Yet it had stood there on the main street, at the core of things, a gathering place, a focus, and its destruction caused a subtle disorientation that would last for several years to come.

Fire had thus struck a second time at the heart of St. Paul's. Unlike the burning of the School House in 1878, this conflagration had no clearly defined cause. The investigations following the fire, the protracted questioning of individual students, created a severe breach in morale. The origin of the fire was never officially determined, and rumors and suspicions were rife.

The fires of 1878 and 1961 both tested the faith of the community. But whereas one had been the result of a stroke of nature, borne with such fortitude as men have always shown when the river rose in floods or their crops were burned, this later one seemed to have been caused by an evil power from within. Coit gathered the strength of the community and displayed his own rugged force in making a fresh beginning. For Matthew Warren, as for other leaders of his generation, the task was more difficult. Not the wrath of a righteous God was to be appeased or suffered with resignation. The challenge was to deal with a culture imbued with contradictory and often self-destructive impulses.

As the troubles of the next decade gathered, that fearful January night would seem to be symbolic of the way communities suffer for reason they only partially comprehend, and from which they recover in ways not capable of being foreseen.

14

Troubles of the Sixties

1964–1969

In the autumn of 1964 Matthew Warren set out on a sabbatical which was to keep him away from the school for the whole academic year. It was a midway point in his rectorship. Up to then he had driven forward in a course of change and innovation, sometimes straining his relations with the Board. He returned to find growing discontent on the part of a student body complaining that he had not gone far enough.

In charge during the Rector's absence were the two vice rectors, Ronald J. Clark and William A. Oates. The former was an enthusiastic teacher of mathematics, a formidable squash player, and a proponent of educational innovations. The latter, who had come to the school under Nash, had risen quickly, emerging from the registrar's office to serve under Kittredge as director of admissions.

These two, in reports to the Rector during his absence, described a school subject to the usual tensions and problems, yet revealing some puzzling aspects. There were significant disciplinary cases, some misbehavior at a school movie, and (as Oates put it), "a bit more freedom of expression" than Warren had been accustomed to—"more willingness to back up opinions with action." It was a picture, seen in retrospect, of a society precariously in balance as it approached the waterfall of revolt.

St. Paul's was in fact undergoing—like many other schools and colleges at this time—a change in mood and temper. A new

youth culture was beginning to define itself. Disillusionment
with the fruits of technology and material progress was spurred
by dramatic events occurring with dizzying rapidity—the assas-
sinations of President John F. Kennedy, Martin Luther King, Jr.,
and Robert F. Kennedy. Meanwhile the ongoing Vietnam war
seemed to validate youth's worst opinions of its elders.

Countrywide, the students' reaction was to withdraw into
their own culture while vociferously denying the values, the
rules, and the traditional forms of the society they inherited.
The still-inarticulate revolt manifested itself in everything from
weird hairdos to the burning of draft cards. Experiments with
drugs became pervasive. St. Paul's was slow to follow, its students being generally isolated and conservative.

Within the school, nevertheless, students began to complain
of restraints which hitherto they had borne lightly. Despite the
reforms going steadily forward since the Drury era, school life
was indeed marked by a web of rigid regulations and prohibitions. In the choice of courses, the ways of spending leisure
time, the opportunities for relationships with minorities or with
the opposite sex, the students—or at least an activist minority
of students—began to see themselves as deprived.

By the mid-1960s something like a revolutionary mood was
developing in Millville. A particularly brilliant group of sixth formers put their mark on the *Horae Scholasticae* and the school's
literary societies; a handful of activists, influenced by politically
conscious, younger members of the faculty, voiced the mounting
mood of dissent. Finally, several strongly individualistic sixth
form presidents were endeavoring to bring St. Paul's into line
with what was going on at other schools and colleges.

The school administration responded to the growing dissi-
dence, not by searching for culprits but by pushing forward with
changes that had been in progress for several years. These included freely granted weekends away from the school, as well as
experiments in reducing the number of compulsory chapel services. Requirements for seated meals, enforced study hours, and
formal rules of dress were also relaxed. At the same time efforts

*Matthew Warren,
as the Sixties moved
toward their climax.*

were made to increase the number of minority students and—not least—to bring in groups of girl students during the winter terms.

In his Annual Reports Matthew Warren stressed the degree to which events in the outside world were affecting the atmosphere at St. Paul's. "The question," he wrote, "is whether we are able to change our habits of thought, our inbred prejudices and predilections, our preferred view of ourselves and our world. We must do so…quickly enough to help our young people live fruitfully and sensibly." "There appears to be no end to the restlessness," he wrote again," and our own community is not, nor should it be, unaffected."

In May 1968, pent-up emotions suddenly blazed out. St. Paul's had always been a place where the word counted deeply, and in this crisis it was words, not acts of violence, that carried the students' revolutionary message. A proclamation, signed by eighty sixth formers and as many from the fifth form, was posted on various bulletin boards (somewhat as Martin Luther had posted his heretical theses on the door of the Wittenberg cathedral). The document was in the form of a three-page, single-spaced letter, phrased with astonishing bitterness.

The school was pictured as a mindless institution, imposing on its members a regime of indignities and oppression.

Old dreams of glory persist—solitary practice on the Lower School Pond.

Students, it contended, were subject to a power structure that allowed no "spontaneity, openness, honesty, and joy." The masters were held to be either obsequious to the administration or withdrawn from the concerns of the boys. The reforms of the past several years were denounced as shams. In short, claimed these dissidents, the students were tired of being politely listened to while their real concerns continued to be ignored.

Matthew Warren was away at a meeting when the students' letter was promulgated. He was infuriated not only by its tone and substance but by the fact that it had not first been presented to him. Nevertheless he refrained from summary dismissals and kept the channels of communication open. A group of the disaffected students was invited to present their case to the Trustees. During the summer months a projected review of the curriculum was transformed into a wide-ranging discussion of every aspect of school life. Eighty sixth formers remained after graduation to help set the agenda, and a representation of students met with faculty members through the vacation.

The academic year of 1968–1969 was, nevertheless, a stormy one. If the immediate crisis had passed, resentment and a spirit of agitation remained. The community had been deeply shaken—boys set against masters, masters against their colleagues. To Warren's lasting credit he kept it from being damaged irreparably. As the students engaged in various forms of insurrection—from adopting outlandish forms of clothing to refusing to stand for prayers in chapel—Warren continued to discuss and to listen. The process was hard. "If heaven is good," he wrote privately, "I won't be made to do it again in this world."

Of the events of the late 1960s it can never be said that they altered nothing. When the ferment subsided, St. Paul's was a changed place. A single-sex school had become coeducational, and minorities made up a sizeable portion of the student body. A church-oriented school had to a large extent become secularized. A relatively narrow course of study had been expanded to offer almost a hundred courses, while the students' field of personal choice had been enlarged in every sphere.

Matthew Warren captained the ship through the storm, but by 1969, approaching retirement, he urged the Trustees to begin the search for a new rector. He himself would leave as soon as they found their man. He had made a supreme effort and he was tired; besides, he felt a younger hand should be at the helm. The Trustees set out on a broad quest, but they found the field narrowing to the school itself. In February 1970, Amory Houghton, Jr., president of the Board, announced that William Oates had been selected. Faithful to his belief that a new rector should take office immediately, Warren retired at the close of that winter term.

He went out with the honors due his extraordinary services. Not always understood by the school constituency, he had carried out his task with immense vision and energy—a reformer, an innovator, a wise counselor of youth, and at the end an undaunted leader through a time of storm. On the morning of Sunday, March 8, 1970, the chapel was crowded for a special service to mark his retirement. The emotions of the hour were expressed within ancient forms—invocations that had been read at the school for a hundred years, hymns that carried their message of hope and of time's defiance. No sermon, no eulogy, broke into the solemn ritual of prayer and music. "O God, thou summonest the prophets and the apostles to speak in thy name and to walk with thee." Thus spoke the celebrant. And the family of St. Paul's responded: "*Halleluiah, Amen.*"

In perspective, Warren stood with the greatest of the school's rectors: with Coit, who had established it; with Drury, who had restored it. No less dramatically than these he had played his part, driving the school forward to meet the claims and expectations of a new age. He suffered the fate of pre-revolutionary leaders—being identified with the old order after having acted powerfully to create a new one. He bore with dignity misunderstandings of his position, strengthened by religious faith and by a sophisticated grasp of historical forces.

At Anniversary 1970. The students wore long hair and dishevelled clothes.

Summing up the Warren years in the alumni magazine, the school's longtime head of the history department, Carroll McDonald, put the matter definitively. That the school withstood, relatively unscathed, the impact of 1968 and 1969, he wrote, "is due to the care with which Matthew Warren rethought the long tradition inherited from his predecessors and to the extent to which he made the school a more integral part of the larger community."

15

Shaping the New Community

1970–1982

William Armstrong Oates, who would prove a strong rector through a period of continuing change, was born in Aberdeen, South Dakota, in 1916. The town had a population of 16,000, and the state was then part of a vanishing rural America. In his youth Oates had traveled to Chicago, but he never went farther east until he formed the determination to attend Harvard College. Aberdeen was to see little of him thereafter.

He was an engaging youth who took advantage of his opportunities and quickly formed friendships in influential Harvard circles. Upon graduating he went abroad for a year on a scholarship and then completed his Master of Arts degree in English. Thus armed, and newly married, he appeared at Shady Side Academy in Pittsburgh to begin a career of teaching. A year later, as a freshman St. Paul's master, he moved with his wife and his eldest son, then three months old, into an apartment at the Upper School.

Under three rectors—Nash, Kittredge, and Warren—Oates had gained experience in all fields of the school's operations. When Warren urged the Board to elect him as his successor, the choice seemed providential. At fifty-four Oates still looked youthful and moved with the brisk air of authority. The death of his wife several years before, leaving him with the care of three sons, left marks on a disposition naturally cheerful and optimistic; but it had not diminished his zest for power.

William A. Oates,
Rector. A strong
sense of authority
under a mild exterior.

Oates quickly took command. In the world outside, opposition to the Vietnam war was fired by the undeclared invasion of Cambodia. Across the country college campuses were in turmoil. The administration in Washington showed itself out of sympathy with youth, and when the National Guard opened fire on protesters at Kent State University in Ohio, the situation everywhere became explosive. At the height of the national crisis, Oates suspended regular classes, setting up seminars in which the underlying issues of Vietnam could be thoroughly discussed. A number of St. Paul's students traveled to Washington to take part in anti-Vietnam protests.

For a while in that turbulent spring, life at Millville seemed to consist of a continuous series of committee meetings. Every kind of issue was broached, from the most broadly international to the most parochial. Older values were scrutinized and challenged, while a host of fresh ideas emerged. It was a fine time to be alive, and the new rector was in his element.

Bill Oates had a way of convincing the young that he was on their side—indeed, that he was suffering as much as they while seeking answers to their problems. Sensitive under his matter-of-fact demeanor, often revealing an unsuspected degree of emotion, he impressed the young with a feeling that everything could be worked out anew, and that in whatever was done a sense of the student's individuality, and of the validity of his personal experience, would be controlling.

He was a layman, yet he could be pastoral in his concern for the individual. He was a pragmatist, yet he guarded the old folkways and symbols. Giving cohesion to what might have appeared contradictory views or actions was Oates' firm grounding in developmental philosophy. Belief that the human being is in an ongoing stage of growth, reaching for a unique vision, provided a moral foundation comparable to that given by religion in earlier

Before coeducation—
fantasy girls.

days—and one that, like Christianity, stressed the values of caring and mutual support. As the embodiment of this philosophy, Oates captured the affection and trust of the St. Paul's students, and largely held them throughout his rectorship.

Beyond keeping the peace, the first preoccupation of the new rector was the conversion of St. Paul's to a coeducational institution. Exchanges with neighboring New England girls schools had laid the groundwork in the last years of Warren's rectorship. Then, without elaborate studies or prolonged discussion, the Trustees voted in the spring of 1970 to admit at the earliest possible time "a substantial number of girls." The enormous amount of detail necessary to carry out this policy was left to the new rector and his aides.

Oates quickly set in place his administrative organization, headed by a quizzical and experienced teacher of English, Philip E. Burnham, and a former head of the science department, John H. Beust. The former dealt with matters of faculty and curriculum, the latter with the budget and the school's physical plant. It was an effective triumvirate—though Oates would never let it be forgotten that he was in ultimate control. Applications from female students arrived in reassuring numbers, and several months before the Trustees had mandated, the first group of girls arrived at Millville.

In debates at Trustees meetings, going back to the beginning of Warren's term, it had usually been presupposed that if coeducation was to be established, it would be in a separate campus on school property. But now, with a minimum of physical changes, the old school itself accommodated the newcomers into various dormitories. The girls were to be part of St. Paul's, equal citizens of the commonwealth.

They represented, these first nineteen arrivals, major strands of the school's past as well as of its future growth. Two African-Americans were among them; a girl from Concord, New Hampshire; descendants of one of the school's founders and of the influential post-Civil War Trustee Samuel Eliot. (The latter girl's great-grandmother had been one of the young women whose visit to the Rectory in 1878 had so entranced the boys.) Such was the little band that now, after St. Paul's had been for one hundred and fourteen years an all-male society,[1] astounded, delighted, and ultimately transformed the school.

The girls had their problems. They were expected to be themselves—while being looked on by several hundred young men as exotic strangers. They were challenged to be competitive without seeming aggressive, and to be friends with each other while not rejecting the friendship of boys. In the beginning there were at most one or two girls in a classroom, and they tended to be discreetly silent. A shyness among the boys they occasionally mistook for unawareness of their presence. In the nooks and crannies of the school there still lingered, indeed, unfortunate residues of speech and habit to suggest that the girls had not ever arrived.

Wisely counseled by an increasing number of women teachers, including Roberta E. C. Tenney and Virginia S. Deane, the girls soon found themselves and made their place at the school. In extracurricular activities and in sixth form leadership posts the girls were soon fair rivals. They showed their proficiency in sports. In field hockey, soccer, basketball, squash, lacrosse, and tennis their teams were often undefeated. They grew in numbers from 114 in the autumn of 1972 to 177 in 1974. Meanwhile, termination of the Lower School as a separate entity (already in process before the girls arrived) permitted the admission of boys to the upper forms at roughly the old rate.

A quest was soon on foot for the widening of relationships between the sexes. The way to this end came to be known as "intervisitation"—the right at specified times for students of one sex to visit the dormitory rooms of the opposite sex. It was argued that the kind of open, caring community to which St. Paul's aspired could only be attained if friendships were based upon knowledge of one another, upon close acquaintanceship and shared experi-

---

1. To be sure, not quite an "all male" society. The Advanced Studies Program held in summer for New Hampshire youths had admitted girls on an equal status with boys since 1961; moreover, Warren (as noted above) had instituted exchanges in 1968 and 1969 for limited periods with two Massachusetts girls schools, Concord Academy and Dana Hall.

A new era. The first nineteen girl students to arrive in Millville,
January 1971.

ence. The matter was a delicate one, and all concerned recognized
it to be so. The Rector took the lead in channeling discussion and
defining options. Prolonged discussions in all forums open to the
school were supplemented by voluminous written reports. It was
Oates' way to listen to all sides, endlessly if need be, and now he
all but drowned the issue in meetings and memoranda.

When in April 1975 he announced in chapel that he had
given his approval to intervisitation and that it would begin
the following autumn, he was, surprisingly, greeted by only
polite cheers. As the *Pelican* explained, the issue had been
talked to death; the excitement had been taken out of it, and
now was the time to get on with other things. That undoubtedly had been Oates' intention. But intervisitation would remain a touchy practice to administer and would be at the
bottom of future agitations.

The "girl problem" being thus effectively disposed of (at

The girls' teams starred in athletics. Ski team 1972 with Roberta E. C. Tenney, coach, at left.

least for the time being), an equally difficult problem remained in regard to minorities at the school. At the root of much of the dissent in the sixties had been a demand of the more socially-conscious students for the admission of more African-Americans and a greater representation of foreign students. In the mid-seventies these pressures were renewed, and St. Paul's made determined, if not always successful, efforts to deal with them.

The black students who were coming in increasing numbers were children of the civil rights movement, reared among urban struggles for equality, and determined to express themselves and their culture. They were not seeking to be part of the Millville community so much as to establish a community of their own. They sought changes in the curriculum, tables apart in the dining rooms, and even their own dormitories. To allay these demands, and at the same time to recognize the rights of these minorities, was not always easy.

In one notable confrontation black leaders (supported by a good many whites) announced they would not wear jackets or ties even in classrooms or in chapel. It was an act of defiance, and Oates dealt with it summarily. He called the students involved to his office. This time there was no patient exploration, no talk of committee meetings or consensus. There was a plain ultimatum. If the minority continued to disregard the rules on dress, the Rector would fire the ringleaders, in circumstances damaging to their careers and their ability to act as future spokesmen for their race.

It was a gamble—and it paid off. Convinced that they had made their point, the students returned to the normal dress code. But a few weeks later (this was like Oates) a relaxation of the dress code was quietly announced, to be followed by a fresh emphasis upon black history in the curriculum.

By the late 1970s blacks and foreign students were making contributions to the community through all the normal channels, in sports, in dramatics, in publications—not least in the leadership of the sixth form. Yet to be black in these years at St. Paul's was not easy for those who experienced it. They launched themselves into a world for which they were ill prepared. They returned to communities that had grown strange to them and where they were looked on with suspicion by their former friends. The published memoir of one such student, *Black Ice*, by Lorene Cary '74, testifies passionately to the trials to which she felt herself exposed. It is honest and it is unforgiving; yet the account does credit to the courage of the author, as it does to the school that managed, all in all, to be tolerant and caring. By her, and by others like her, St. Paul's was given at least as much as it gave them.

The dark side of the St. Paul's in the nineteenth century was the rigid application of rules and constraints—a system which Joseph Coit had characterized as close to militaristic. In this latter half of the twentieth century the scales tipped the other way. The dark side was persistent failure by the students to live up to the school's expectations in matters of conduct and behavior—dealt with by disciplinarians generally humane and even lenient. The social upheavals of the 1960s, the breakdown of traditional moral and sexual standards, the prevalence of drugs and alcohol contributed to the local unrest. The world was at Millville's gate; its pressures and influences could not be stopped there. What was happening throughout educational institutions, public and private across the country, was bound to affect students at the school.

Waves of vandalism and stealing, and, even more ominously, of substance abuse, confronted St. Paul's throughout the Oates years. He dealt with these problems as a thoughtful, enlightened man. He was sure that repression was not the key, but the offender's deeper engagement in a vital community life. He encouraged the formation of a "spirit committee" to combat "boredom and apathy." Forms of "creative rowdiness" were invented—such strange entertainments as volley ball bombardments, hall hockey, and human pyramids. One winter week in which the Spirit Committee had been particularly involved received a rave review in the *Pelican*. "It was wacky, it was a week to remember." It fomented a happiness "that spread to those desperately in need of it."

On another level, students were encouraged to address the problems of peers who returned to the school after suspension. Sympathetically, they led the reformed culprit into constructive and absorbing projects. If he had sinned out of boredom, explained an optimistic scribe in the *Pelican*, he (or possibly she?) would discover that "spending an afternoon stoned" was the true boredom.

The disciplinary committee served as a forum where individuals could have their cases heard by a small group composed of teachers and students, with each infraction considered by itself and against a wide background of considerations. At the same time the administration increased the level of professional counseling and brought in outside experts on a regular basis.

Amory Houghton, Jr., Board president, with the Rector.

Underlying these practical moves lay Oates' developmental philosophy. "Human activity," he wrote in a characteristic vein, "is almost never single in its motivation. We look behind the actions to understand the life of the individual...Our response [to disciplinary problems] is to the controlling forces behind the action, rather than to the action itself."

As for rules and codes, Oates argued that the school "should frankly accept opportunities for living within ambiguous situations without asking to render all issues precise and clear." In this spirit the administration of justice should be a matter of learning, a part of the educational process itself. The students accepted this approach cheerfully enough, finding that it gave them ample freedom without imposing an excessive sense of responsibility.

Meanwhile, at another level, the Trustees were busy. The 125th anniversary of the school was approaching, and it seemed that something appropriate must be done. Why celebrate it at all? inquired one writer in the *Pelican*. Why not wait

New times, a new atmosphere at the school.

for a good, round 200th anniversary—or at least a 150th? The anniversary the Trustees were now contemplating was a nondescript milestone. It didn't even have a Latin name. Some sort of celebration nevertheless seemed warranted, and the Trustees decided on first, a big fund drive, and second, a scholarly initiative which particularly enlisted the Rector's enthusiasm.

The Fund drive took the name of "The Fund for SPS" and was set at a figure boldly conceived to meet the needs of the school for the next several decades. The drive for $30 million— as large as the school's total endowment a few years previously—was under the chairmanship of Samuel R. Callaway. Assisting him in laying out the grand design of the drive, as well as taking care of its innumerable details, was Robert Duke, who was then serving also as director of development at the school. A sharp fall in the stock market cast serious doubt on the timing. But the drive went forward, and at the end of six years, in January 1980, it was announced that the goal had not only been reached but surpassed.

An early fruit of the fund-raising was a pledge of a donation to build a performing arts center at the school. Interest in the arts had burgeoned over the decade, stimulated by the emphasis on personal development and more particularly by the arrival of girl students. The pledge was not honored, but encouraged by other gifts, the Trustees decided to proceed with the challenging concept—a series of related buildings where dance, music, and drama could be staged. The firm of Hardy, Holzman and Pfeiffer, well known for their work in the contemporary style, was commissioned. They recommended a site removed from the school street (where the performing arts might have been expected to find their home) but closely integrated with the academic center.

Adoption of this suggestion was significant. Oates, strongly supported by the faculty, envisioned the performing arts not primarily as a leisure activity but as part of the regular curriculum. The leadership taken by the Rector was acknowledged when, at a dinner marking his retirement in 1982, the Alumni Association established in his honor a fund of $100,000 to be used for development of the performing arts. Moreover, in 1992 the performing arts center was named for him.

The new theater was completed in 1978. It was in the form of a "black box," attached to the rear of Memorial Hall, where difficult acoustics and an inflexible proscenium stage had handicapped major theatrical productions for years. For the opening, *A Midsummer Night's Dream*, produced and directed by students, made full use of the new theater's possibilities, whose stages and seats for the audience could be rearranged at will, and where actors ascended and descended on all sides. Two years later the music building opened, providing practice rooms and a hall admirably suited to small concerts and solo performances. The dance building gave a new dimension to the classical and modern dance program, which under Richard Rein's direction had been developing since the early 1970s.

As for other plans for the 125th, Oates had proposed, and now pursued avidly, a cooperative venture with *Daedalus*, the publication of the American Academy of Arts and Letters. A scholarly reexamination of American secondary education was to bring together outstanding educators and scholars at seminars in Cambridge and in Concord.

The pageantry of the occasion was not, however, to be neglected. On April 6, 1981, the Rector and his wife rode down the school street in a horse-drawn carriage, invoking memories of the arrival of Henry Augustus Coit and his bride just 125 years before. The president and vice president of the sixth form sat in for the two boys who accompanied them. No dog, unfortunately, could be persuaded to come on board. This somewhat awkwardly reenacted scene, indicative of the Rector's willingness to make use of myths and symbols when they seemed useful, was to precede other events of that anniversary year.

It was presumed that the celebration would take a traditional form, and much speculation surrounded the choice of a speaker. It was difficult to imagine anyone suited to so grand an occasion. One young member of the Anniversary committee took it on himself to propose that, since Henry Kissinger had allegedly declined, the only possible substitute was the Lord God Almighty.[2] The Anniversary, our scribe opined, would cost a good deal of money, and having a speaker like God could well help repay the investment.

In the end it was not a speaker, but convocations connected with the *Daedalus* project, which gave the occasion its distinction. Conferences at the school in the spring and autumn of the anniversary year brought together figures of wide repute and provided the school family, along with assorted guests, a unique opportunity for intellectual stimulation. The two resulting issues of *Daedalus*, devoted, respectively, to the public and the private schools of America, stand as important documents among recent educational literature.[3]

The Anniversary was the last major undertaking of Oates' term. Thereafter his days as Rector were numbered. He did not change his pace or surrender any particle of power. The daily

---

2. The author of this piece was Charles Scribner III. He was later to become a Trustee of the school.

3. The two issues of *Daedalus* sponsored by St. Paul's School are: Summer 1981 and Fall 1981, vol. 110, no. 3, and vol. 110, no. 4 respectively. Especially noteworthy is the article in the latter by the sociologist Sara Lightfoot which gives a revealing picture of the school at that time.

Bill Oates, with his wife Jean, cuts the 125th Anniversary cake.

schedule continued to the end. He would arise at earliest dawn, work at his papers, and read until eight. He would be in his study in the Schoolhouse until eleven, and then go off to Concord, where he would have a leisurely swim. After lunch he was to be found in his study again. There, with two afternoon breaks, he would dictate and fill appointments. The first break was, understandably, for a nap. The second was for a walk with his wife, Jean, which took him down to the playing fields and into every corner of the school domain.

At the farewell dinner which the alumni gave him in New York he said little—as he said little at any other time—that revealed his private thoughts. He left Millville in June 1982, retiring to a house on the Maine coast. Departing, he greeted his successor only in the doorway, and reentered the Rectory but once or twice in the years that followed.

16

The Goodly Heritage

1982–1992

In 1980 Ronald Reagan was elected President of the United States, and for the next twelve years, under Republican leadership, the country passed through a period of relative calm and stability. The mood and spirit pervading the national scene was to come over the little community at Millville. After the turbulence of the sixties, after the host of residual problems dominating the seventies, St. Paul's sought a return to old ways and values—to the assimilation, under tradition-sanctioned forms, of the broadened liberties painfully won. Patriotism and family were watchwords of the Reagan years; at St. Paul's the emphasis was on reaffirming the religious base of the community and on rethinking the meaning of its past.

The process of readjustment began at Millville in September 1980 when Ralph T. Starr, a long-standing Trustee, read on behalf of the Board's president a letter announcing that Oates would retire in June 1982. The news in other circumstances might not have been startling, scarcely seeming to warrant so formal a presentation. Oates would be sixty-five in that year. He had served twelve years since Matthew Warren's withdrawal to his seaside home in New Hampshire. Moreover, there was a clear understanding that faculty, including rectors, retired at sixty-five.

The matter, however, was not quite that simple. With the exception of Kittredge, who needed no encouragement to lay

down the long-borne burden of leadership—who was un-
abashedly pleased, indeed, to be turning to a life of relaxation and
ease—the rule had never been applied to rectors of the school.
They had died in office, left for other jobs, or retired early by their
own choice. Oates appeared ten years younger than his sixty-odd
years and his energies were undiminished. He obviously enjoyed
his work. Every aspect of the school he knew intimately; every
fork and turning in the exercise of power he had mastered.
Moreover, a former vice rector, Ronald J. Clark, had recently
failed to retire at the appointed age. "One year at a time," he said
jovially of his future plans, and on another occasion let it be
known that he would take his leave when any member of the
Board of Trustees could defeat him on the squash court.

That Oates should placidly go along with the age limit was,
in the circumstances, a surprise to many.

The students spoke of him fondly as the Great Administrator.
They admired his efficiency; they knew that under his brisk exterior was a human being who understood their problems.
When he didn't agree with them, they accepted the fact re-
signedly. At the end of Warren's term, when the search committee was seeking qualities desired by students in their next rector,
one had replied that, whatever else, he should not be "a father-
figure." To be a father-figure would be "a kiss of death." There
was never any danger that Oates would be that; but he could be
like a sympathetic friend or a wise family counselor.

With the faculty he was not equally popular. They chafed
under his strict control of all decisions. Perhaps increasingly, as
his term advanced, he became an I-am-in-charge-here sort of
rector. A certain impatience extended to his dealings with the
Board of Trustees. It was said, only half in jest, that he never entered a Board meeting without a letter of resignation in his
pocket. So it was that some of the faculty felt that his retirement
was not altogether untimely.

Searchers for a new rector cast a wide net. The school family watched curiously as mysterious strangers walked the

grounds, evident candidates for the post. Indistinguishable from the others at that time was a tall, lean figure, benign in appearance and courtly in manner. He was none other than Charles H. "Kelly" Clark, dean of the Berkeley Divinity School at Yale. Somewhat later, on March 8, 1982, he and his wife Priscilla entered the school chapel amid loud applause. Then rector-elect he toured the domain where he was to rule for ten years. Students noted approvingly that he appeared "laid back" and very relaxed.

Clark had spent his life within the Episcopal Church. Born in New York, he moved as a boy to California, where he attended The Thacher School. He served in the ministry of missions of the Episcopal Church, spending twenty years in the Far East—in the Philippines and Singapore—before returning to Yale, from which he had been graduated. His wife shared enthusiastically in his work—an excellent singer, an adept conversationalist, and the best actress among rectors' wives since Gertrude Kittredge. They were the parents of five children.

The new rector conceived it his mandate to re-awake the school's religious tradition; to strengthen the sense of its being a home—"an almost perfect home" in the words of the first Coit; to increase faculty participation in decision-making; to be economical; and to channel change within accepted forms. He began quietly, as was his manner. The most obvious change he brought about was in the chapel services. Oates had used the services as community gatherings, as a stage for the acting-out of student fantasies and for the expression of their artistic and intellectual talents. A layman, he saw the need for religion's emotional outlet.

With Clark, however, religion was at the core of life. If he aspired to set a mark upon his rectorship, it was as the beloved pastor, the true shepherd of his flock. The memory of his years is treasured now, not because of his command over events but for the profound sympathy, the generosity of spirit, with which

*Charles H. (Kelly) Clark,
the ninth Rector.*

*James W. Kinnear III, president
of the Board, Anniversary 1987.*

he carried the school family through good times and times of trouble or bereavement.[1]

Significantly, he found in the Old Chapel the ideal stage for a new religious expression. It was not that the vast spaces of the Chapel of St. Peter and St. Paul fazed him. On great occasions he could put the congregation under his particular spell. He loved the music of the Chapel's superb organ, the movement of the crowds of young people entering and leaving, the bright color streaming through stained glass windows. He was himself a striking presence. His unforced tones reached to the most distant worshipper. As a preacher he had few equals among the school's rectors.

Clark had no expectation of being able to fill the big chapel on a voluntary basis, nor was there any thought of making Sunday services once again compulsory. It was enough that "two or three"—and hopefully a few more—should gather together in the Old Chapel. For the smallest congregation he would prepare carefully. Often the limited numbers seemed in fact to intensify the religious experience, and even to extend it outward, touching in some unseen way the life of the school beyond.

At year's end the sixth formers gathered here as they had done in the time of the first rector, intimately, under a mysteriously potent force; and on these occasions Kelly Clark made of the old building a true shrine. In the years of his rectorship the little chapel, once condemned by the Trustees to destruction, was lovingly restored, and a plaque at the entrance linking Clark's name with that of Henry Augustus Coit gave him a great deal of pleasure.

The students responded in their own way—variously, as it is with the children of this world. If few were converted, many were impressed. It was difficult to see a man so obviously believing in what he said and preached, a man whose life seemed grounded so firmly in a faith eluding them, and not be put into

---

1. Clark's deep personal involvement in one tragedy shared by the school is lovingly recalled—the death by accident of Jonathan Tracy, son of George Tracy, admired teacher of English and long-time head of the classics department. An open-air theater by the Library Pond is dedicated to Jonathan's memory.

Clark brought a reaffirmation of religious values. In the sacristy of the Chapel, 1987.

a receptive mood. If the percentage of students attending Sunday services did not noticeably increase during Clark's rectorship, a fresh current was felt in the school—a greater tolerance for, and perhaps interest in, religious values. When the *Pelican* summed up the first year of the new regime, it spoke warmly of the "soft-spoken and sincere manner of the Rector."

Yet, true to form, the editors added that such changes as Clark had brought about were "met with a gamut of emotions, from appreciation and affection to opposition and resentment."

Within the Rectory, where Bill Oates and his wife Jean had established open-house for all students on Saturday nights, there was, the *Pelican* added, "a new tone and a new cuisine." These occasions had become important in student life, and Oates liked to say that he had missed only one of them during his years in office. As many as three hundred students would attend during the three-hour period, to be greeted by their hosts as they entered and left, each with a word. As many as a thousand chocolate-chip cookies would be regularly consumed, along with ten pounds or more of cheese.

The Clarks, with their numerous offspring, restored to family use the downstairs rooms of the Rectory, largely treated as public spaces during the previous administration. Students were received on Saturday evenings into the privacy of a home enriched by personal and exotic touches, especially objects recalling the Clarks' many years in the Orient. As for the "new cuisine," it was the fruit of a special talent of Priscilla Clark, who later gathered her recipes in a popular cookbook sold for the benefit of the school's Missionary Society.

Clark was fascinated by the school's origin and evoked it on every possible occasion. These Saturday evenings at the Rectory recalled to him the earliest days, when Henry Augustus Coit and his young wife gathered the school's first students around them for conversation and reading. As part of the school's 125th Anniversary the Trustees had asked the author of this volume to write a modern school history. Published in 1980, it received scant notice in Millville, where the anti-historicism of a developmental philosophy prevailed. But Clark read the book before accepting the rectorship, and afterwards drew from it his vision of the school. It was said that he "re-invented Millville." Indeed he made the first Coit seem his daily mentor and his constant companion.

Clark altered drastically the centralized way in which the school was administered. He did not particularly enjoy wielding worldly power. In this sphere, as he remarked later, there was "an awful lot of sharing." Faculty meetings became forums where anyone felt free to express an opinion or to propose a course of action. The making of decisions was widely distributed. If the school ran on smoothly, it was because he had at his right hand an experienced administrator, the vice rector John N. Buxton, and because he had the wisdom to give Buxton a loose rein. It could be said that the administrative system put in place by Oates was never dismantled; its control was handed over to the vice rector. Clark remained at the top, as much the priest as headmaster—"the bringer of peace," as an admiring colleague put it, "the bringer of decency, the bringer of love."

Clark was not to escape the nagging problem of discipline at the school. Indeed as his term progressed, it came more and more to occupy center stage. Beginning from different roots, he arrived at an approach not dissimilar from Oates': an emphasis on understanding each individual; a resolve to treat infractions of the school rules as part of the total learning process. The rules, moreover, were not to be cast in concrete but to consist of generalized expectations of the way young men and women should behave in a good community. Clark saw the students as "growing into fullness of life," and was inclined to be patient with their experiments along the way.

To an outsider it might appear that these young people existed in a kind of Eden, children of "the goodly heritage" and beneficiaries of enormous gifts of caring and of material endowments. Could they not show the simple decency of conforming to what the school asked of them? But Clark was not particularly surprised by their defections. He could view the school in biblical terms. There was always the "Serpent" in Eden; and there was also, he never despaired of believing, a God: "walking amongst the woods and by the waters of Millville."

What youth saw was their own intensely personal struggle to grow up, in an environment where rules existed to be tested and a functioning individuality was the ultimate objective. Relations with their peers was part of the search, as was a dangerous toying with chemical substances. "We're teenagers," one of them wrote. "In fact we're not particularly remarkable teenagers. We're apt to make the same mistake eight or more times. Sometimes (horror of horrors!) we don't take things seriously."

Amid these crosscurrents Clark navigated, on the whole shrewdly, helped by a discerning and deeply-probing disciplinary committee. The system worked well enough, but the students found themselves in a state of some confusion. "We are all dumped into the expectations cauldron each fall," was the way one of them expressed it. But when more conventional methods of discipline were tried, the student response was apt to be highly negative. Room-searches were "an unspeakable breach of trust." Locks on the doors (to counter a wave of petty thefts) "would halt the stealing. But locks would do nothing to halt the deterioration of our school's ideals."

A particular offense against discipline was known as "cruising"—being outside one's dormitory after hours. It was an infraction touching the most sensitive aspects of student life; yet it was difficult to enforce, as it was to devise for it appropriate punishment. A *Pelican* writer treated the matter facetiously. Admitting a certain concern that "the cruiser might freeze to death," the writer saw nothing else wrong with the practice. Cruising was judged a quite normal reaction to stress and a release of nervous energy. Some might indeed cruise for the purpose of entering other dormitories or meeting "other people," but mostly it was done "for the love of freedom and of nature."

Unimpressed by such arguments, the administration reinforced the security guards on the campus at night. The response was another salvo from the *Pelican*, a straight-faced report to the effect that the Trustees had taken a drastic measure. They had decided to delay the main work on the new library (then under construction) and to give priority to a high-windowed tower at the building's east end. Books could wait; indeed to the Trustees books were less important than a watchtower. A watchtower would make security more efficient and save the the guards from looking ridiculous as they chased teenagers around the campus. High-power sweep-lights were to be installed in the tower within the week, and a megaphone system would soon follow, keyed to harmonize with the chapel bells.

All this was in the background of a landscape otherwise sunny and placid: too sunny to please some of the more cynical. "St Paul's School has a very intricate camouflage system," a student explained in the *Pelican*. "The school hides problems from the outside world, and we hide problems from the teachers, each other, and ourselves." The majority of students, however, were ready to take things as they were. Like generations before them, their life was a busy round of classes, extracurricular activities, and spells of escape from the school's routine. Early in his administration Clark had initiated one more review of the curriculum. Small but significant adjustments were made in almost every aspect of the school's life, many of them in schedules and priorities, designed to lessen the stress and haste to which many felt themselves prey.

Somewhat paradoxically, in a period when personal relationships and subjective concerns played so large a part, the performing arts and public speaking continued to flourish. To the delight of all, the Rector and his wife both took part in school plays. The dance department enlisted not only ambitious and talented girl students but some of the best male athletes. The music department grew into its new facilities, diversifying its offerings to a point which would have seemed unimaginable in days when the chapel choir provided the only serious opportunity for the musically gifted.

The Hugh Camp Cup for public speaking had never been more avidly competed for. In a single year as many as fifty-five students of both sexes tried out for a chance to address their peers. To be sure, the subject-matter of the speeches was different from former days—more often abrasive or dissenting, sometimes intensely personal, with few orators treating politics or national events.

Debating, far from dying out, had become a highly popular activity and one for which St. Paul's was famous throughout New England. Under a dedicated coach, E. Lawrence Katzenbach III, the school teams had cultivated a style and attained a mastery of rhetoric setting them apart. Year after year they carried off the championship in region-wide contests. Their hallmark was the use of music stands instead of a podium in debates, the lightweight transparent support underscoring their independence of notes or texts. Also, they liked to think, the music stands intimidated their opponents.

New buildings were few during the Clark years. It was like

Cast members of "Noye's Fludde." In the chapel, celebrating the building's hundredth year. Mrs. Noye, Priscilla Clark, seated center.

him, and in line with his mandate for economy and simplicity, that improvements took the form of restorations, rehabilitations, or additions to existing structures. (The new library, as will be noted, was a grand exception.) "Friendly House," once the home of female servants, was remodeled to make a dormitory and named Warren for the seventh rector. A resource center in Payson, the science building, donated by the family of John Franklin Enders (SPS 1915 and Nobel Prize winner); rehabilitation of the Chapel of St. Peter and St. Paul along with restoration of the Old Chapel; a dramatic renovation of the Upper School; and finally, after more than fifty years of hard use, the rehabilitation of the Schoolhouse—these were not negligible (nor inexpensive) undertakings. Even to the *Pelican* such enlargements and renewals gave little occasion for complaint. The cantankerous bird could not withhold, however, a wry comment on work being done on the Schoolhouse. "Hard to swallow," it opined, was replacement of stones in the much-used stairway. "Steeped in tradition and stept [*sic*] on by the soles of generations of toiling Paulies, the absence of their soft concavity will cause many sleepy students to stumble."

To the Rector, repair of the Chapel was perhaps the most satisfying. A careful survey of the building's physical needs coincided with plans for marking the hundredth anniversary of its erection. Clark wanted to use the occasion as a reaffirmation of the school's religious tradition, and he followed the work with close concern. For a year, indeed, no other develop-

Dance took a major place among the performing arts. Philip Neal and Sarah Davidson, 1985.

ment at the school seemed so completely to occupy his mind. In the summer of 1987 he visited in Berlin the studio of Dr. Hans Gottfried von Stockhausen, commissioned to design the new stained glass window depicting the Parable of the Sower and the Conversion of St. Paul, with a border of mustard vine. The last to be installed in one of the two bays added to the chapel in Drury's time, its installation and dedication were a high point of the centenary celebration.

The crowning new work of the decade was, of course, the Ohrstrom Library. Sheldon, the old library dedicated in 1901, had for many years been inadequate, designed for a school of three hundred-odd students pursuing a limited curriculum. Not only was there scant space for books; there was—at least until the damp basement was cleared for makeshift carrels—insufficient space for study. For twenty years the need for a new library had been debated, formally and informally, and the discussions usually ended with no one being able to decide whether books had a future. By the mid-1980s it was sensibly agreed that books and computers would each have its place in the new learning.

Serious fund-raising for the project began. The Trustees commissioned Robert A. Stern, a leading "post-modern" architect whose son had recently graduated, to undertake the work. Stern sited his building between the school street and the Lower School Pond, forming a great quadrangle open to the pond and contained on two sides by the old and the new chapels. He incorporated into the structure references to buildings he found about the grounds—the turret, already alluded to; the chimney of the Powerhouse; and added to the roof the kind of shingle "eyebrows" which might have been found in a New England train station. The building was noble in scale, fit to balance the great chapel of Henry Vaughan, and was sumptuously detailed and furnished. On its completion in 1991 it received wide public notice and was considered by many to be the architect's finest work.

On December 12, 1990, the Rector sat in a corner of the old library reading to a cluster of students the last stave of Dickens' *A Christmas Carol*. "Then finally," as the Rector de-

The Ohrstrom Library.

scribed it, "we stepped out into the starry windless night while the lights of the old building were extinguished and the doors were locked and closed behind us." A few days earlier a chain of students had begun to move the books to the new library on the other side of the pond. The old stood dark and unused until a few years later, splendidly restored, it opened its doors to a new life as center of admissions, development, alumni affairs, and school publications.

The formal dedication of Ohrstrom Library took place in April 1991. It was a "damp day," which means in Millville that there was plenty of rain. The ceremony had to be held indoors, in the Chapel of St. Peter and St. Paul. An address was delivered by Vartan Gregorian, President of Brown University and former President of the New York Public Library. A prayer was pronounced jointly by the Bishop of New Hampshire and the president of the school Board. The chief donor, for whom the new library was named, George L. Ohrstrom '45, was on hand, as were others who had contributed generously to the completion and furnishing of the imposing structure. The librarian, Rosemarie Cassels-Brown, observed the ceremonies and then got quickly back to the work of making it a vital force in the daily life of the school.

From these pleasant scenes we must return to problems of student behavior. In the spring of 1990 students found that their huts and forts in the woods had been torn down. Such flimsy, informal structures had been part of the school tradition since the nineteenth century, alternately frowned on and tolerated by successive school administrations. Like the practice of "cruising" they were defended by the students as being an expression of "love of nature and of liberty." (The "liberty" in this case seems to have left traces in beer cans and cigarette butts.)

Some new force was evidently at work within Clark's genial realm. When on May 6 a meeting to discuss discipline was called in Memorial Hall, students were quick to state their case. "Many of us chose this school because of the generosity of its limits," the editors of the *Pelican* asserted. "They knew this was a school where the individual was trusted. Why are we changing our ways now?"

The following autumn the *Pelican* commented on "the greater clarity with which the school has articulated its intended responses to breaches of expectations." In other words, rules were being defined and penalties were being made clear in advance.

A change in atmosphere, subtle but nevertheless pronounced, can be attributed to developing apprehensions among members of the Board of Trustees. Convinced that St. Paul's was lax in discipline, they found their concern fanned by a variety of factors. The country was in a conservative mood and not prepared to tolerate youthful offenses. Large fund drives, bound to be affected, were on foot within the school constituency. Moreover, New Hampshire laws governing sexual behavior were strict, and the school could claim no immunity from them.

A detached observer within the school later gave it as his opinion that in the two decades 1970 to 1990 disciplinary standards had not declined and that, if anything, they had improved. That is not the way it was seen within the Board or by many outsiders. A chapel talk by a highly respected faculty member addressed the problem. "For years," the speaker declared, "St. Paul's has had to live down a reputation as 'a party school.'…It is a reputation at odds with the facts, but it is a reputation which has dogged us year after year." Whether or not this view was correct, the Rector was certainly under pressure to tighten up on the enforcement of rules.

By 1990 the question of Clark's successor was under discussion within the Board. Simultaneously there impended a change in the Board's leadership. James Wesley Kinnear III had been president for twelve years, serving ably even while fighting off a hostile takeover of the large company he controlled. Now he followed established practice in making it possible for a newly-chosen president to preside over the selection and installation of the next rector.

When Kinnear resigned as president, Kelly Clark lost a faithful and affectionate supporter. For the remaining two years of his term, Clark was subject to growing criticism. In his last Annual Report as Rector he defended himself outspokenly. "If I have seemed visionless to some," he wrote, "in my reluctance to support those who have advocated certain distinct if not radical changes in the school's programs and methods, it is only because…I have found them wanting, at least from my point of view and for the time being."

The obvious choice to succeed Kinnear as president was Walker Lewis. Outstanding president of the sixth form of 1963, Lewis had gone on to found a highly successful Washington consulting firm. Elected to the St. Paul's Board in 1970, he was already, at the age of 27, an outstanding presence. The lucidity of his presentations based on charts and figures impressed even his most venerable colleagues. Looking to the future of the school, he saw disturbing trends; and he was not always in-

Walker Lewis, newly elected president of the Board in 1990, with Kelly Clark.

clined to draw optimistic conclusions. "He was one of those men" (as was said of Judge Samuel Huntington, among the school's original Trustees) "who when they take hold of a thing are apt to shake out its folds." Active, decisive, habituated to promoting reorganizations, Lewis satisfied the desire for vigorous leadership shared by a majority of the Board.

One of Lewis' first acts as president was to form a planning committee with authority to look into all aspects of the school. To its head he appointed Dr. Randolph Guthrie, a fellow-Trustee who had been a strong voice for change. Guthrie was energetic, impulsive, generous of his time and money; but he could also be brusque and tactless. His highly organized inquiry caused resentment and confusion among the faculty. Lewis may have come to regret his choice of Guthrie, but for the moment the two men worked in harness as they made plans for the choice of a rector to succeed Clark and, more broadly, to bring about changes in the school's life.

Evidence that St. Paul's was losing its competitive edge was now joined with a conviction that circumstances placed extraordinary responsibilities on the school. During the decade the endowment had grown at an unprecedented rate. Generous contributions, including a bequest of Adolph Rosengarten, Jr. (largest ever received by the school), had been astutely managed to bring the total by 1992 to the astonishing sum of $227 million. Walker Lewis, in particular, saw the school under a charge to use this endowment for novel and creative purposes. It was not enough that in its relative isolation St. Paul's should provide a place where students could find themselves and be happy. The school must sharpen its focus and step out boldly to be the leader in a new age.

Priscilla Clark at the dedication of a rowing shell named in her honor; with David V. Hicks.

17

Three Crowded Years

1992–1995

Kelly and Priscilla Clark had been loved at St. Paul's. The decade-long influence of Clark's rectorship had penetrated and suffused the school's life; his quietness, decency, and good faith had created an atmosphere palpable to the least sentimental of students and faculty. In saying goodbye to Clark the students were aware of entering upon another era, one less lenient and less tolerant of their frailties.

For two years, as the previous pages reveal, the students had been aware of a changing attitude on the part of the administration. They did not necessarily attribute this to the Rector; they could always blame the head of the disciplinary committee or the vice rectors. But they braced themselves against the arrival of the new incumbent. And so the 1992 Anniversary issue of the *Pelican* was a generously affectionate farewell to the Clarks, while hinting that the golden age was over.[1]

In October of the previous year the rector-elect had made his first official appearance at the school. David Hicks was a striking figure. Younger than any on taking command except

---

1. Kelly and Priscilla Clark retired to an historic house close to Long Pond. Devoutly the former rector ministered to a small congregation in nearby Dunbarton, taking pride in the thought that Henry Coit had often preached there. In 1993–1994 he served as interim minister to Manhattan's famous St. Bartholomew's Church on Park Avenue. It was the small Chapel and the big Chapel all over again!

David V. Hicks,
the tenth Rector,
Parents Day 1993.

Coit and Drury, vigorous, articulate, poised to speak plainly, he was a man clearly not afraid to draw lines and to spark controversy. The impression he made on this visit was judged by the *Pelican* to be generally favorable, but the students detected what was to many of them a disconcerting emphasis on "hard" subjects—the classics, science, mathematics.

When first approached by the Trustees, Hicks had not been inclined to enter into competition for the post. He was in every fiber of his being an educator and a reformer, and he questioned in his mind whether St. Paul's was ready for his style of leadership. A graduate of Princeton and a Rhodes Scholar, he had been for fourteen years headmaster in two different schools in the South.

He was the author of *Norms and Nobility*, a well-received book setting forth a coherent educational philosophy. That he could realize his vision within a school so traditional as St. Paul's seemed to him doubtful. But in the end, and after other possible candidates had been eliminated, he was persuaded by Walker Lewis and by Winthrop Rutherfurd (chairman of the search committee) that the Board was serious in their commitment to change.

The Board had not been idle while the search was progressing. Two months after Lewis had assumed the presidency the first of fifteen meetings of the planning committee was held in New York, each running some five hours in length. Selected members of the faculty were grilled. Outside experts were called in. Every aspect of school life was examined, including areas not normally the immediate responsibility of the Board. The aim of this reexamination was, first, to guide the Trustees in the choice of a new rector, and then to sketch out steps they thought it was essential he should take. A final meeting was held at Guthrie's ranch in Wyoming in the winter of 1992, with rector-elect Hicks present, along with two trusted consultants long familiar with the school—Oates, the former rector, and Duke, former vice rector.

Hicks' mandate for change in the school's social and educational life was thus confirmed—a mandate more explicit and more far-reaching than that of any previous rector-elect. By the same token the Board was set to engage itself directly in a broad range of current issues. The results were to play themselves out in dramatic circumstances.

When Hicks and his family settled in Millville in the autumn of 1992, the students found him easy to talk to, ready to listen, and were impressed by his "rectorial voice." Ellen became part of the faculty, teaching English. At the Rectory, now enlivened by three young children and several cats, the custom of open house on Saturday evenings was continued. Nevertheless, the sense of impending change hung over the scene, disturbing faculty and students alike.

The chief worry of the students was in regard to intervisitation. The privilege of being able to visit in the rooms of the

David and Ellen Hicks as newcomers to Millville.

opposite sex during specified hours had been established during the Oates administration and was treasured as a basic freedom. That some new limitations would be imposed was accepted as more or less inevitable, but when Hicks addressed the subject in a chapel talk early in his first term, he knew he was treading on dangerous ground. Where Clark had moved cautiously, merely asking of the students a higher degree of responsibility, Hicks came to the hard conclusion that coed visiting would no longer be allowed during afternoon hours when the dormitories were unsupervised. He spelled out his reasoning in a long talk, discussing in detail matters which were already well understood by the students. They were not happy with the tone or with the substance of the announcement.

The situation was not not helped when the text of his talk was distributed to the entire alumni body. Recent graduates were dismayed by a curtailment of privileges which they had gained and guarded. Others were disconcerted for a different reason—it shocked them to find the subject of sexual relations discussed openly and candidly at their old school.

Ellen Hicks conducting a mini-class on Parents Day 1992.

The faculty, meanwhile, had its own worries. Committed to new forms of interdisciplinary studies, Hicks was determined to fill vacancies with teachers believing in this approach and prepared to pursue it aggressively. In the early months of the new administration, before the plans for curricular change were fully understood, seeds of apprehension sprouted widely; and even when compromises and adjustments had been made, many retained strong doubts. A morose spirit, fanned by vehement commentaries in the *Pelican*, spread through the community. At the same time, a small group of sixth formers—for reasons of their own—engaged in distressingly anti-social behavior, until the school family (including the editors of the *Pelican*) cried Shame!

David and Ellen Hicks could well look back upon their opening term as a disappointing one. "For headmasters," as the Rector remarked in his Annual Report for that year, "the first year is notoriously difficult." But there were no complaints from him. He pursued his course as one accustomed to taking conflict in stride, convinced that a man can learn from mistakes and profit from victories postponed. He had work to do, and he was resolved to do it despite misunderstandings and setbacks.

The essence of this work was forecast in the conclusions reached by the planning committee. Distilled into a series of "challenges," they were to be converted by the administration into "goals." The Rector assured the school that faculty and students would be involved in shaping the new program. With his top aides he then moved quickly to implement them, launching a series of committee meetings which dominated school life over the early months of 1993. Some complained, indeed, that in the long hours of debate—leading gradually to compromise and growing consensus—not only was the faculty being worn down but that student instruction was being neglected. If he could not please everyone, Hicks showed that he could be patient and searching. When a statement of Goals was brought before the Board at a special meeting in the summer of 1993, it was accepted without prolonged discussion.

What were these "goals" by which the future of St. Paul's was now to be shaped? In number they were fifty-eight (undoubtedly too many!); they touched every aspect of school life and learning—from a radical revision of the course of study to the inculcation of good sleep and study habits. They proposed modifications in the composition of the student body and changes in the way students and faculty lived together in residential houses. They stressed the adoption of new forms of technology as aids to learning and new emphasis on science and classics. Within the overall scheme everyone could find something to favor—and almost everyone, too, could find something to dislike or to fear.

More important than the specific proposals was the vision that underlay them. That vision was Hicks' own. He saw a school with many ways different from that which had been developing over the recent years. He envisioned one where graduates would be inspired to active service in the community where they live; marked by a striving for the kind of perfection sought by Athenians in the classic age. He saw a school drawing the best youths worldwide and yet—because the school was essentially a family—appealing to the sons and daughters of graduates. Keyed to the unfolding future, its members would be articulate in its many languages—"from our own noble English tongue" (as he declared in an address to the Millville Society) "to Newton's calculus and Euclid's geometry, from the Greek of Plato to the New Testament, to Einstein's physics and Escher's teasing art"; and they would be overlords, too, of the new techniques of research and communication.

He saw a school that, like all truly good schools "unapologetically and proudly name their values, honor their gods and heroes, pass their judgments, and defend their faiths....They tolerate many things but some things they will not tolerate....They seek the eternal knowledge of God's truth and man's destiny, along with those lofty ideals and exacting standards for daily life that Aristotle called 'virtues' and that cannot be destroyed by a simplistic belief in 'progress' or by ideological notions of 'political correctness,' however well-intentioned."

It was a large vision, and in some ways a stern one; but no one familiar with the history of St. Paul's could doubt but that Hicks was recalling what seers of its own past had dreamed and had pursued.

With immense energy, Hicks set forth to implement the new program. Again committees were constituted and cooperation sought. Several smaller changes could be effectuated promptly. Least easy—and a top priority—was the shaping of a revised curriculum. This called for the abolition of several of the older departments and the formation of new divisions centering on the humanities, the sciences, and residential life. The first of these courses, Humanities, was introduced in the third form in the autumn of 1994. Drawing together English, history, art history, and religion, it enlisted students for lengthened classroom periods of discussion and analysis of carefully selected texts, in an atmosphere where the lines separating teaching and learning were blurred, where clear expression in the spoken and written word was emphasized, and where fresh relationships were established between traditionally discrete areas of study.

A cornerstone of the new program, dear to the Rector's heart, was the interdependence of the school's intellectual and dormitory life. As Jefferson had conceived his academic village at the University of Virginia, and Woodrow Wilson at Princeton had fought to establish residential colleges, Hicks believed that only in the right atmosphere of living could studies be fruitfully pursued. A core of studies entitled Residential Life was prepared for introduction in 1995, while the course in Humanities was extended into forms above the third, and Science, Mathematics, and Technology was being developed as a new division.

The delicate and complex process of formulating these curricular changes took place, unfortunately, amid occurrences that shook the administration and sharpened divisions within the Board.

Robert Duke had been a significant figure at the school—twice vice rector in charge of development and architect of the successful fund drives of the 1970s and 1980s. He had been deeply involved in the negotiations bringing Hicks to power. A highly regarded consultant to major New York institutions, Duke was now invited back to serve for a year as vice rector while a permanent director of development was being sought. With his wife, Tommie, he arrived at Millville in the autumn of 1993.

Hicks viewed his new colleague as the best possible man to raise funds to implement the school's ambitious goals. Among Trustees, with many of whom he had close ties, Duke was seen, rather, as one who would advise and oversee the administration. Misunderstanding doomed the initiative from the start, and when a disgruntled Duke packed up and left in December—he did not resign, it was said, and he was not fired—his action intensified all the strains that had been building up.

Many of the school's teachers, already disturbed by curricular changes, gave way to their worst apprehensions. A standing committee of faculty leadership solicited unsigned comments on David Hicks' record. About half the faculty responded, and of these a majority expressed themselves as "unhappy with the Rector's personal and management style." The faculty then sought access to the Board. Postponed from the regular winter meeting to the spring, the matter was ultimately dropped. Due to restraint on both sides the issue of Hicks' rectorship was never formally posed.

At the same time, factions developed within the Board. Guthrie, who had been an enthusiastic backer of Hicks' appointment and was a confirmed advocate of educational changes, turned against the Rector. Submitting to his colleagues a complex and minutely detailed list of dissatisfactions, he demanded Hicks' resignation. The confidential document was leaked to the faculty and presently was being received in unmarked envelopes by prominent alumni. The Board leadership stood firm, but divisions of opinion and conflicts of loyalty caused several resignations. A number of influential alumni, old friends of Duke, were seriously disaffected.

It has occurred repeatedly in the history of the school that when the Trustees are divided, the organized alumni forcibly exert their role. It was so in the declining years of Joseph Coit, as it was under Ferguson, and in the first turbulent Drury years. It proved to be so again as Walker Lewis struggled to reestablish the unity of his Board. The Alumni Association awoke from twenty years of relative somnolence and under the presidency of Albert F. Gordon and his successor Coleman P. Burke demanded a higher degree of recognition, more numerous representation on the Board, and, in particular, control over the alumni magazine.

The *Alumni Horae* had long been a primary means by which the school administration projected its image of St. Paul's, not only to the alumni body, but to the wider public. Drury had strongly objected to its being "kidnaped" by an organization outside of his control. Now the issue was posed again. Walker Lewis complied with alumni demands, but not

A happy dedication ceremony in the courtyard of Kehaya House, 1994.

before a further resignation had shaken his ranks.

It was a hard time for Walker Lewis, who fortunately was undiscourageable and never wearied under the burden of leadership. It was a hard time, too, for David Hicks. He was striving to implement reforms in line with what the Trustees had urged and for which he had won a large measure of general assent. Yet he was operating in an atmosphere heavy with mistrust. In January 1994, in a personal memorandum to the Trustees, he concluded with words that do credit to his courage and his essential decency: "Personally…this is a period of pain and concern—but not of self-doubt—for me. I do not believe it is either a surprising or a bad thing that we should be here. These fears and negative feelings—bottled up—are much more dangerous over the long run than their release is now. I must respond attentively and sensitively…"

The spring of 1994, as spring has a way of doing in Millville, brought a welcome brightening of the scene. A handsome new dormitory donated by an alumnus, Ery Kehaya '42, was dedicated in a delightful ceremony. Applications for admissions were up for the first time in several years (though the number of alumni-related applicants was down). An above-average number of students admitted early decided to stay with their first choice. As a result the school would open in the fall

After winning the Reading Regatta, the SPS crew went on to win at Henley, 1994.

crowded to the last place. The Parents Fund and the Fiftieth and Twenty-fifth Anniversary Funds all set records. Moreover, Dr. Guthrie eased tensions by resigning from the Board.

The most unexpected boon was still in store. It was a victory glorious on its own and symbolic of the way an institution—especially an institution composed of the young and the high-spirited—can find itself anew as in an act of grace. The first boys' crew in that spring was recognized as being a strong contender in any competition it might enter, but because several of its rowers would return the following year, it had been decided to wait a season before sending it to Henley. However, the crew defeated all rivals in the New England championship held at Lake Quinsigamond in Worcester, Massachusetts. Thereafter there was no holding back. On the historic Thames in England St.

Paul's won the Marlow and Reading regattas, and on June 2 swept to victory in the climactic contest for the Princess Elizabeth Challenge Cup at the Royal Regatta at Henley—the only American crew in history to win all three regattas in one year.

Eton, most formidable of rivals and holder of Henley records, had been eliminated by St. Paul's in the Henley semifinals. Two days later, still feeling the strain of that supreme effort, the crew from Concord had outrowed by a length and three-quarters the American championship crew of Atlantic City (New Jersey) High School.

Coached by Rich Davis and Chip Morgan, captained by Amory Blake and Charles Koven, with Decker Rolph as stroke, the crew had achieved what was undoubtedly the greatest season in the long history of St. Paul's rowing. For this, year after year, crews had sweated at the machines and frozen in the mist-laden airs of early spring training. For this, when the waters of Long Pond were denied them, they had carried boats to the muddy, brush-obstructed Turkey River. The moving scene of Shattucks and Halcyons coming down in horse-drawn barges to the flagpole on Race Day—so many generations, so many victories and defeats!—all seemed to culminate in what a handful of rowers accomplished during those days in far-off England. Moreover, there was something representative and redeeming in the crew itself, in the diversity of its members, in their modesty, their generosity to defeated rivals.[2]

The victories on the Thames may have marked a turning point in a difficult time at St. Paul's. But something like its characteristic cheerfulness had never been entirely lacking from the school scene. While contention played itself out in various circles of the community, students were busy with sports and studies; putting on plays, staging ballets, engaging in debates and in a variety of literary and artistic activities. Indeed, the *Pelican* some-

2. A hardly less splendid victory, though a less glamorous one, was won by SPS the following year, when, after again winning the New England championship at Worcester, the crew journeyed to Cincinnati, Ohio, to attain the national championship, competing against crews from all over the United States.

times appeared to be telling tales of two separate and unrelated worlds—one reflected in the gloomy columns of editorials and opinion, the other in vivacious pages devoted to sports, the arts, the comings and goings of stimulating or inspiring school visitors.

In the late autumn of 1993, when things seemed at their darkest, David Hicks wrote a long letter to parents giving his account of what had recently been taking place in the life of students. It was as if he was seeking to reassure himself that beneath the day's problems the currents of the traditional St. Paul's still swept on, carrying young and old, teachers and students, on their healthy, life-affirming swell.

He described what would have seemed a remarkable abundance of riches at any point in St. Paul's history. "We enjoy the cultural life of a small city," he wrote, "and the talents of a vital and involved community." Two striking exhibitions had been mounted in the Hargate gallery. A production of *Mother Courage and Her Children*, with an original musical score performed entirely by students, set standards that would be hard to surpass in the future; while the ballet corps staged a brilliant *Nutcracker*. A stream of visitors had come to Millville, several of them staying long enough to engage in discussions and classes with the students. These included a writer and photographer from the French newspaper *Le Figaro*; and two friends of a young female AIDS victim, who before a large audience in Memorial Hall described her short but fulfilled life.

Public speaking and debating had been enthusiastically pursued, with Timothy Barsky '94 the winner among orators, for the first time in the long history of the Hugh Camp Cup carrying off the victory for a second consecutive year; and with debaters sweeping the annual Exeter tournament without losing a single match. Meanwhile, a bewildering array of sporting events was unfolding. For the first time a football game was played under lights—on a Saturday on Concord's nearby Memorial Field, with almost the entire school cheering from the sidelines as the home team triumphed over St. Mark's. Other varsity football events were not always successful,

*Students expressed themselves freely during the
period of change.* Pelican *editors Max Lamont III
and Tom Champion, 1995–1996.*

*Student actors Jennifer Jones, Dana Goodyear, David Coggeshall, and
John Harden perform scenes from the Latin play* Curculio *in the
Jonathan Tracy Memorial Theater, Anniversary, 1991.*

Champion girls field hockey team in action.

though the team played hard and in a climactic game held off for three and a half quarters the physically much heavier Belmont Hill team before succumbing to a heart-wrenching defeat.

The girls' soccer and field hockey teams, both varsity and JV, turned in a string of victories; the girls' and boys' cross-country teams were alike outstanding. So the story went—ups and downs, glories and disappointments; but always the zest of the game played for its own sake. "Truly," concluded the Rector's letter, "we have much for which to be thankful."

In a 1994 fall issue the *Pelican* struck a note not recently heard: "The year has been extraordinarily successful in terms of morale here on the campus." Perhaps there really had been a change in climate. For the first time since David Hicks' coming, the leadership of the school was passing to students who had not been present during the Clark regime. The fabled congeniality of that era was now indeed only a fable to them. They could accept the present with its invigorating—if sometimes chilling—breezes;

they could take David Hicks as he was, without fear and with growing respect. If Drury had been the prophet in power, and Henry Kittredge the happy teacher, Hicks was the personification of the schoolmaster—dedicated, professional, bold. The students complained that he did not remember their names, but he understood them in general, and he was passionately committed to shaping conditions in which their lives might be well lived.

They sometimes seemed to speak a different language, these young people and their demanding chief; and misunderstandings were bound to occur. When the Rector framed a formal document entitled "The Trust," setting forth the school's expectations, students found the word "trust" being used in a way quite alien to them. Trust to them implied that they be discreet (especially where relations between the sexes were involved); to show good taste in their choice of options; to be unobtrusive in their shortcomings. David Hicks wanted to be able to trust them to refrain from sexual intimacies and, in fact, to rise above most human failings.

The dialogue was bound to be interesting, and in the end the idealism of youth on the one side, and the wise forbearance of the schoolmaster on the other, were certain to bring about some sort of rapprochement. It was difficult to discount the Rector's message, when he spoke with the authority of humane learning, expressed by the ancients and tested by the experience of two thousand years. When he asked of the young that they "live responsibly and with self-restraint," he was speaking for the best of the classical and of the biblical inheritance; reminding them that "the moral life cannot be imposed from without by means of prohibitions, but must grow from within, inspired by worthy norms and meaningful relations," he was coming close to the heart of beliefs that St. Paul's had lived by, both in old and in modern times.

How shall this narrative end? In histories there is no end. There is only change and development; only what subsequent generations judge to be progress or apprehend as decline. If St. Paul's moved successfully along its chosen path, it would emerge as an institution not only relevant to its age but

Old traditions persist—view from the Chapel tower of post-graduation farewells.

an example to which others would turn for inspiration. But if it fell short? No one dare speak dogmatically of the future of any institution—least of all of one that stands poised so delicately between the hopes of youth, the concerns of their elders, and the unrelenting pressures of society.

So the last word goes fittingly to the great rector of the school's middle years. "We live," said Samuel Drury, "and we work, by faith." Drury surely meant faith in a transcendent power. Those of a later day can say humbly that their faith is in each other, in the destiny of the school, and in the kindly Providence that has favored it thus far.

THE END